TEN CENTS TO PROSPER
THE GATEWAY TO VISION

Fred Wyatt

Copyright © 2007 by Fred Wyatt

TEN CENTS TO PROSPER
THE GATEWAY TO VISION
by Fred Wyatt

Printed in the United States of America

ISBN 978-1-60266-639-9

All rights reserved solely by the author. The author guarantees all contents are original and do not infringe upon the legal rights of any other person or work. No part of this book may be reproduced in any form without the permission of the author. The views expressed in this book are not necessarily those of the publisher.

All scripture is King James unless otherwise noted. Copyright © 1986 by World Publishing. All rights reserved.

Bible quotations are taken from Amplified Bible (AMP). Copyright © 1954, 1958, 1962, 1964, 1965, 1987 by The Lockman Foundation.

The Message (MSG). Copyright © 1993, 1994, 1995, 1996, 2000, 2001, 2002 by Eugene H. Peterson

CONTENTS

Introduction
    Why You Need This Book? 7

Chapter 1
    A Thief and A Liar 13

Chapter 2
    The Covenant Connection 25

Chapter 3
    The Purpose of The Tithe 37

Chapter 4
    The Key That Unlocks 55

Chapter 5
    Why Tithe 69

Chapter 6
    The Boy Who Believed in The Tithe 85

Conclusion 94

Tithers Prayer 101

Questions Regarding The Tithe 105

TEN CENTS TO PROSPER
THE GATEWAY TO VISION

Introduction

Give, give, and give. That is what we always hear. Everybody wants money. Everybody wants a dollar. Give to the children's fund or the church building project. When will this cycle of everyone wanting our dollar end? Or, is it your local phone carrier asking for ten minutes of your time? We live in a society that is high tech, fast-paced and money-driven. The mighty dollar rules everything around us. It causes good guys to turn bad and turns saints into sinners. What is your motivation? Why do you work? Even if you do have a good heart and you donate to cancer research, would you give money to someone you couldn't see? As hard as you work, could you really give away something to someone you've never met? Maybe, but it would be hard. I would like you to take a journey with me to meet my God, a God that supplies and offers total provision.

Tithing may very well be one of the most debated subjects among Christians. Tithing is not only a biblical principle that causes you to be blessed, but it also causes the church (the Body of Christ) to prosper. It is a sensitive subject because it deals with the touchiest subject of all, money. Here are a few questions that will provoke you to go beyond your usual thought patterns and tap into the core of why you do what you do. Brace yourself while we go a little deeper. Do you believe in tithing? If so, why do you tithe? If you don't believe in tithing, what is the basis for your decision? I'm not interested in what you were told; I want to know what you believe. What series of truths have shaped your thinking? What have you learned that motivates you in your decision making to accept or reject tithing? How much does tithing matter to God, and how is it tied to His plan for your life? Okay, now that I've poked and prodded, are you squirming yet? If so, then we're just getting started because discomfort is a necessary stop on the road of truth. You see, I have learned that discomfort is good if it leads you to the truth.

    Tithing was foreign to me for most of my "church going" life. Countless Sunday mornings were spent sitting in a pew, but no one ever explained to me that tithing was a Biblical principle. Pastors, teachers and leaders were all around me, yet no one took the time to explain why God commands that His children tithe. Based upon my limited knowledge, asking me about tithing would have been the same as asking me about space shuttles. I didn't know anything about the subject. When I first came to Christ, I was excited about learning about my Savior. I wanted to do all that was required of me to leave the life of sin I had just offered up to Him. Then one day, I heard someone say that I was supposed to give ten percent of my earnings to God. While I had no problem with the calculations, it was the covenant connected to the tithe that I truly did not understand. I did not agree or disagree; I just needed some help clarifying the matter. My request to God was simple, "Can you please explain it to me so I can make the proper decision whether or not I am required to give ten percent?" So I began to tithe based on obedience putting the questions behind me, for the time being.

    Many years later that same question came back to haunt me. It was accompanied by other questions that were still swirling around in my head. I admit that this is one of those subjects that make you go "hmmm". I privately wondered, "Am I tithing because it makes me feel good or maybe because my pastor told me to do it?" If I am not a consistent tither, is it still tithing? Are there any real benefits of tithing? Would I recommend tithing to someone else? Is it an Old Testament principal that no longer applies, or does the New Testament support tithing? All of these questions represent issues that the average Christian has never considered, which is why God gave me the insight to write this book. This journey began when I asked God one simple question, "Why should I tithe?" Although I was tithing when I posed this question, I was never provoked to address the real reason behind my decision. I needed to settle this issue in my heart and in my mind. I just accepted the principle of tithing upon hearing my pastor preach it. From that moment, I started tithing and never looked back.

Then I began to seek God to talk to him about doing things out of revelation as opposed to tradition and religion. I had a strong desire to know more and to operate in the Spirit. I knew that there was more, more revelation, more increase, and more impartation. I was yearning for more. God said what He always says to me when I feel this way, "Come follow me." Usually after those instructions, He takes me down a path of scriptural insight. When I travel down this spiritual path, I never return the same. I am always changed after sipping from God's cup of wisdom. I prayerfully asked God to allow me to drink of the cup so that I might receive the revelation knowledge to minister truth to the Body of Christ. This useful and informative book will not only answer questions as it pertains to tithing, but it will also put you on the path to your destiny, back to the garden which is the original place you were designed to be.

The principles that are outlined in this book are designed to help you tap into the supernatural vision of God so that you will be able to download directly from the source, just like Adam did when he named all the animals. My goal is to provoke you to a hunger that will guide you into seeing things God's way. No matter how hard truth is stomped to the ground, it will eventually rise to the top. It is my intent to present a non-arguable case that God's will is for all his children to tithe. Tithing gives God's children insight to prosper so that the work of the Kingdom can go forth. I want it to be unquestionable in your heart, which will lead the way to captivating your mind. As you read along, allow God to minister to your heart and soul. Pray the following, "God open my eyes to the truth, show and tell me the truth Lord." There are a lot of "truths" but only one real truth. Everyone pretends to have all the answers, but all truth comes from the Creator of all. I encourage you to open your heart to take an inside look at God's thoughts on the tithe. My intent is not to satisfy or try to change the mind of those who aren't seeking the truth. Instead, I am passionately interested in those who are seriously seeking God's will with their whole heart. Remember, you believe with your heart not your head. Your mind must, in order to digest this knowledge and imprint it on your heart. My hope is that when you're finished reading this book, it will make sense to your inner being. I pray you read this not just dissecting, but discerning what is God's will. It is my prayer that this revelation will reach you where you are and bless you and your household abundantly

Chapter One:
A Thief and a Liar

There are many misconceptions about tithing. To have a misconception means to interpret incorrectly, to have your ability to conceive altered. Nothing causes you to interpret more incorrectly than deception. Deception is Satan's biggest weapon. Deception is a lie, and Satan is the father of lies. Think about it, how can Satan steal, kill, and destroy (John 10:10) a believer who has been given the authority to dominate, unless he first deceived them? Take a look at what he did to Adam and Eve. The downfall of mankind began with Satan's deception. Genesis 2:16-17 states, "And the LORD God commanded the man, saying, of every tree of the garden thou mayest freely eat But of the tree of the knowledge of good and evil, thou shalt not eat of it: for in the day that thou eatest thereof thou shalt surely die."

God gave clear instructions for Adam and Eve, in the garden, not to eat of the tree of knowledge of good and evil. Their disobedience to God caused man to lose his rightful position of dominion in the earth's realm. Genesis 3:1-7 tells us of how this deception took place.

Now the serpent was more subtle than any beast of the field which the LORD God had made. And he said unto the woman, Yea, hath God said, Ye shall not eat of every tree of the garden? And the woman said unto the serpent, We may eat of the fruit of the trees of the garden: But of the fruit of the tree which is in the midst of the garden, God hath said, Ye shall not eat of it, neither shall ye touch it, lest ye die.

And the serpent said unto the woman, Ye shall not surely die: For God doth know that in the day ye eat thereof, then your eyes shall be opened, and ye shall be as gods, knowing good and evil. And when the woman saw that the tree was good for food, and that it was pleasant to the eyes, and a tree to be desired to make one wise, she took of the fruit thereof, and did eat, and gave also unto her husband with her; and he did eat. And the eyes of them both were opened, and they knew that they were naked; and they sewed fig leaves together, and made themselves aprons.

The Bible says the serpent was subtle, meaning cunning or crafty. Imagine how good he has become with the same old tricks after thousands of years. Notice how Satan always presents a form of godliness. He quotes scriptures better than a Bible scholar on a memory scholarship. He always takes the truth and twists it around, just one little word or one little compromise. That is why you see millions of people around the world who profess Christianity, but bear little fruit. They are void of a passion for the things of God. They will pray over their food, dedicate their babies, and even call on the name of Jesus, but their lives lack the tangible evidence of a true relationship with God. Satan is raising a generation of powerless pretenders. These are people who look and smell like a Christian, but in all actuality, they are just imposters.

In Genesis 2:8-9, God proposed a question to all of mankind, when He asked Adam, "Where art thou?" Where are you really? It is a question that refers to your present physical location as well as your actual state of mind. Are you really where God has called you to be? Are you tending to the garden that God has given you or have you been eating from a tree of deception? Do you really know who you are and what you are capable of doing? Are you truly happy and totally fulfilled? Do you have enough provision in your life?

In order for there to be an inward transformation, there are many other factors or variables involved. However, the condition of your heart is the most important variable. Ephesians 3:20 tells us that God is able to do "...exceedingly, abundantly, above all we can ask or think," this is made possible by the power which already resides in us, it is according to the power that worketh within you! When Eve sinned she already knew right from wrong, like most of us do. However, she did not have the Word in her heart, it was only in her head. This is how Satan was able to deceive her, just like he is deceiving many today.

In this dispensation, we are witnessing preachers who deliver a message that sounds good, one that sounds like the truth, but it's a lie. The origin of truth must be found in the source of truth, which is God, the Creator. The only way to find God is through his Word. That's why the Bible says,"...study to show yourself approved unto God" (2 Timothy 2:15) not man. God is the one you should be obeying. When you obey God then you don't have to worry about breaking man's law, because God's ways are pure, holy, and righteous. The Bible says the woman saw that the tree was good for food. She saw with her physical eyes instead of her spiritual eyes. The reality is you don't see with your eyes you see through your eyes. You don't see things the way they are, you see them the way you are. Eve allowed Satan to change her perception of what God had already spoken. As we all know, this was a huge mistake.

As believers in Christ, we have been deceived. Satan has attempted to deceive us with the lie that tithing is not Biblical. Why give your money to a God you cannot see? Do you really believe you will be cursed? Many biblical scholars and Bible intellectuals declare that tithing is an Old Testament principle. As they make this false declaration, Satan, the master of all deceit and treachery, has deceived them.

The revelation in your mind is no good until your spirit man imprints it on your heart. Once it becomes imbedded in your heart, it is woven into your everyday life. Tithing should be a way of life for every Christian man and woman.

> I Chronicles 28:9 states:
> And thou, Solomon my son, know thou the God of thy father, and serve him with a perfect heart and with a willing mind: for the LORD searcheth all hearts, and understandeth all the imaginations of the thoughts: if thou seek him, he will be found of thee; but if thou forsake him, he will cast thee off for ever.

You serve Him with your heart by submitting your mind. Your will is in your mind, but that's another book. There are many who don't want to know the truth. They won't tithe regardless of what God says. They would prefer to argue and debate God's word than submit to it.

For too long, Satan has stolen what belongs to God's people. This is not a sob story because we have allowed it. It's not his fault that we don't study to show ourselves approved. We have been listening to grandma and grandpa's old theology about the way things are supposed to be, instead of pressing into the Word of God. It's not his fault that we have placed our favorite TV or radio hosts' words over God's word. We have been failing as sons and daughters of the Almighty God.

Now is the time to rise above all obstacles and carry the Gospel forth like never before. God designed man to have dominion over the earth. He gave Adam and Eve complete dominion over the earth. Once God gave Adam dominion, his authority was permanent provided that he obeyed God. Adam and Eve disobeyed by eating of the tree and the consequences of sin entered the world. Adam owned it all, from the dust of the ground up to the gateway of heaven's doors. We were in line to own it all until Adam and Eve sinned in the garden. Not only did Adam and Eve sin against God, they gave the ownership of it all to Satan. They gave up the keys of dominion to him and the result was a spiritual death. From the time Eve ate of the tree until Jesus came, we were under the grip of spiritual death. Adam went from being able to download divine revelation to having access to mere information. He literally turned over the keys to the Kingdom. Satan convinced Adam and Eve to take from God's portion. The tree of knowledge was God's portion not man's portion. Man took from God's portion, and it caused us our rightful position in the earth. Just as Adam and Eve took from God's portion, those who don't tithe are still robbing God of his portion, the tenth. Our position was to dominate the earth. Even after Jesus came to redeem us from this curse, many are still forsaking their dominion by robbing God of the tithe.

I remember fasting and praying and God telling me that mismanagement of money was the number one sin among people, especially the church. Mismanagement is the same as failing to be a good steward over the things that God has blessed you with. I have learned that being a good steward is critical to the believer's ability to experience the abundance God intended. A steward is someone who has been trusted with something that doesn't belong to them, such as money. Remember, we own nothing and God owns everything. Nothing on earth belongs to us, except our free will. Over twenty percent of the Bible talks about money. So it makes perfect sense that God would set in place some guidelines for a subject of this magnitude. Principles such as tithing, offerings, firstfruits, and making a vow, relate to showing God your faithfulness through stewardship.

Even in writing this book, I am worshipping God through my stewardship by utilizing the gifts He has given me. In an effort to make an impact that will change the world, I have asked God to help me convey and impart what He has given me. Just as my life has been changed by great men and women of God, your life can also be changed. As you are reading, an impartation will take place that will allow you to see in the spiritual realm. God desires that we have both physical and spiritual sight. No longer will your sight remain stale, but it will be unlimited through the wisdom of God. What I am sharing is not an enlightening theory or enticing words without the name of Jesus. This is wisdom digested through one of God's vessels to feed those who are hungry. May you digest the wisdom of the tithe that will cause your sight to be supernatural.

My intentions are not to tear down, but to build up the Body of Christ. It is imperative that you understand that the truth is sometimes hard to digest, however, you will become stronger if you accept it. There are many beliefs and fallacies concerning the tithe. Through the deception of Satan and the lack of knowledge, many are living beneath their privileges. Depending on your religious background, there are those who don't believe in tithing at all. Some religions tithe and don't even know why. Less than six percent of churchgoers worldwide actually tithe. I grew up in a traditional Baptist church and was never taught tithing. In many instances, it was always pay your dues, which I have yet to see in the

Bible. Man-made customs such as paying dues is what Satan has put in place to deceive many from their blessing that God has put in place. He doesn't care about you going to church as long as he can get you into error and neglect the principles of God. Applying God's Biblical principles is the first step towards becoming prosperous.

I began tithing immediately after I became serious about the things of God. I just accepted tithing as the truth and did it. I had received some teaching on how much to tithe, but there was never really any depth to help my understanding. I was always taught God wants only ten percent, which leaves you the other ninety percent to manage. There was nothing wrong with what I was taught, except my understanding was very limited. My limited understanding of tithing prevented me from bearing the proper fruit. In other words, I had the belief and the faith to tithe, but not enough understanding to put the devil to shame. I'm hoping that I can cause you to have an internal transformation as a result of a firm understanding of the tithe. When you bear fruit internally, it will also manifest externally.

It grieves my spirit to see how incorrect teachings are rampantly being taught in churches. As a result, people have become lost in a lie, looking for a return from a system that is foreign to God's system (the Kingdom) or God's way of doing things. Our adversary's goal is to convince the church that the world's system is the only way that will lead to riches. Most people, particularly Christians, don't even know that God designed a system for them to prosper, a system that He put in place for them to succeed. It's almost like putting dimes in a machine that says "quarters only" and wondering why the machine is not working. You have failed to comply with the requirements of the system. Now you can see how a lack of knowledge of God's divine plan causes His people to perish. The world's system will produce only a worldly harvest, that has the world's baggage attached to it.

Applying God's principles will allow you to change monetary systems and move to a place where the rewards are endless. This book is for people who are looking to make a shift in the spirit supernaturally. I would rather sow (deposit) into a fail-proof system where my results are guaranteed, than to invest in a system where money becomes my master. I want you to be free of thoughts of money. Just think, what could you do or who could you become if you never had to think about money? If all you had to do was focus on becoming who God wanted you to be, who could you become as an individual? We have thousands of churches and millions of people with no power, due to the wrong information and poor teaching. When I say no power, I mean they have the appearance of being spiritual, but bearing no fruit.

If you have ever attended a church where tithing was taught, you may have heard the following scriptures in conjunction with explaining the tithe.

Malachi 3:8-11:
Will a man rob God? Yet ye have robbed me. But ye say, Wherein have we robbed thee? In tithes and offerings. Ye are cursed with a curse: for ye have robbed me, even this whole nation. Bring ye all the tithes into the storehouse, that there may be meat in mine house, and prove me now herewith, saith the LORD of hosts, if I will not open you the windows of heaven, and pour you out a blessing, that there shall not be room enough to receive it. And I will rebuke the devourer for your sakes, and he shall not destroy the fruits of your ground; neither shall your vine cast her fruit before the time in the field, saith the LORD of hosts

This scripture is widely used and abused by churches trying to convince or force people to tithe. You may say, how can you abuse it if it's in the Bible? Isn't it the Word of God? Yes, you are absolutely correct, it is the Word of God, but it is only part of the information. Using God's word without explaining the origin behind it, does not do it any justice. Many churches use this scripture because it's the easiest scripture in the Bible to use to scare people into tithing. You will be cursed with a curse if you don't tithe. Yes, that is true, but it still doesn't tell me why. I understand that if I don't bring the tithes in, I will be cursed, but the revelation comes when you understand why you are cursed. When you tell people they are cursed without explaining why, it causes people to flee from church instead of coming to church.

Revelation of God's word is essential because knowing scripture without the proper revelation can cause you to be ineffective in your Christian walk. Failure to give proper teaching on this subject has caused many not to tithe and those that do tithe to miss the revelation of the benefits of tithing. I have found that when tithing is properly taught, you equip the saints with a clearer understanding, which makes it easier for them to release the tithe. I understand that there are those who will not submit to the word no matter what. However, the majority, if taught properly, will conform to God's word. As for the pastors who don't teach or believe in the biblical principle of tithing, I pray that you read this with an open heart and mind, allowing your spirit man and not your intellectual mind to guide you in your future walk with God. Let me explain, what I mean, when I say that the scripture in Malachi is misused. When studying Biblical text there are many factors that must be taken into consideration. You must look at whom God is speaking to, why he is addressing them, what is he addressing them about and when and where this is taking place. You cannot use a scripture out of context and expect the people to be blessed without proper revelation of what God is saying. That would be the same as using the scripture that says women can't speak in the church. You have to understand the culture and the times to understand why that was written and know that in today's society, that is not culturally correct or acceptable. So this widely used scripture in Malachi has God's heartbeat and his thoughts in it, but all the while you have to look at who he is addressing and why. This scripture by itself does not uphold tithing, because technically this scripture is under the law and we know that Jesus came to release us from the law. So there are other scriptures that we must cover to get to the bottom of where God originated the words in Malachi to get a true and firm foundation in your tithing walk.

Once again, the blinders must be removed, because it is the devil's plan to keep the Body of Christ in the dark to the complete truth regarding the tithe. It is a lot easier to obey God when you understand His ways and His Word. The Word of God is alive. It has power and gives power to those who use it right. I am not saying this scripture is not a valid scripture for tithing because it is. Actually, it is a very important scripture where tithing is concerned because it helps you to understand God, his ways and thoughts on tithing. However, it does not address the fullness of the subject. It's a car with two wheels, eyeglasses without lens; it's a house without a foundation. Something is just missing. I had a good pastor friend who invited me to teach on giving to his congregation. To his surprise his tithes and offerings shot through the roof. Why? People were exposed to the truth. Most people want to know the truth and will attempt to do right if given the opportunity to do so. This was not the result of me being such a good speaker as it was the result of delivering the spoken word of God and the truth about the biblical principle of tithing. The increase came because the scales were removed from their eyes and their incomes increased therefore their giving increased. They were shown scripturally how to tap into the vision and revelation of God. There is so much truth that has not been revealed in the area of finances, that it is hard to impart it all in one sermon.

Chapter Two:
The Covenant Connection

Now let's look into the principle of tithing with some depth and spiritual insight. What is the tithe? A tithe is nothing more that one tenth, or ten percent. Yes, it's that simple. Ten percent of ten dollars is one dollar. The tithe off $150 is $15 dollars. Now that you understand the tithe, you should be ready to start tithing today right? Let's dig a little deeper. The tithe is ten percent of your gross income, not your net (which is what Uncle Sam gives you after taxes). I don't want to get technical because we are not under the law but let's stick there for now. The origin of the word tithe is from the Hebrew word "ma'aser" meaning tenth. Some may ask, "Can I tithe my time or my furniture in place of money?" The answer is no, you cannot. You can give your time or furniture but it's not considered as a tithe before God. God wants ten percent of your income not other things. I will explain why as we continue into the Word.

God's Word is full of principles. Give and it shall be given. The law of sowing and reaping is another example. These are all principles that when applied properly, the results are guaranteed. A principle is a basic truth or law, a procedure established by authority, (I love that one), a fixed or predetermined outcome. God has established laws or principles in the earth. These are the principles we as believers in Christ are to live by. They are not get rich quick schemes. Oral Roberts would say, "Methods may change, but not principles." Scholars who talk of tithing always rely on the Levitical priesthood of tithing. This is fine but it is not the origin of tithing. Old Testament scriptures are used solely to justify tithing as just a practice of the Old Testament, which is not reliable. When people try to make tithing exclusively an Old Testaments principle and say that the New Testament command is to give, not to tithe, then people believe they are released from the burden of obeying God. With this type of flawed theology, Christians are free to give only when and if they feel like it as opposed to the way God intended. God desires that you give, and do so abundantly, but the tithe is required of you for many reasons.

The origin of tithing started with a man named Abraham, not the Levites as some may believe. Abraham is called the father of our faith. Abraham was the man that God called to bring his son Isaac to the altar to slay before God. Out of his obedience to God his son's life was spared. Prior to God's request that Isaac be sacrificed, Abraham's name was Abram. However, God knew his expected end and called him Abraham, which means father of many nations. This was a transitional period in his life because God had called him to birth nations out of his loins. So God required a new, fresh anointing on his life to carry out such a task. Abraham is critical, not just in tithing, but also in your entire walk as a Christian. Abraham is not just an Old Testament figure but also a patriarch in our walk as Christians today. His legacy reaches much further than just the book of Genesis in the Bible. God told Abraham that He would make out of him a great nation (Genesis 12:2). He also promised him that he would give him all the land to possess and to his seed forever (Genesis 13:15). God tells us in Galatians 3:29 that we are Abraham's seed and an heir according to the promise that he made with Abraham. So everything that God promised to Abraham, is also promised to every believer.

Abraham was a prophet of God who not only saw things to come, but understood things as they were. What good would it be to know the future if you didn't understand how to walk with God in the present? Covenant is a right now thing. Who honors this covenant? Why is it honored? What is covenant? Where is the covenant used? These are great questions deserving great answers.

To get the true revelation of tithing you must first understand the word covenant. Covenant is a term that actually means, to cut. It is an agreement between two or more parties ended only by death. For example, a handshake made in blood would signify a covenant between two people. Another example would be the breaking of the hymen of a female virgin. The breaking of the hymen would cause blood to flow, which signified a covenant between a man and a woman. Which is why sexual intercourse is reserved for the union of a husband and wife in marriage. (In the Old Testament, a father would give his daughter to a man and upon the consummation of the union, a man would know if she was a virgin or not based upon the breaking of the hymen. If the woman was not a virgin, she would customarily be stoned to death.)

A covenant is the strongest binding agreement known to man. If the world understood covenant there would be fewer divorces, more blessings and more obedience towards God. Who honors this covenant? If a covenant is made between two people, then each individual is responsible for honoring his part of the covenant. There were many covenants made between God and man but none were more important than the one God made with Abraham. God made other covenants such as the covenant with Adam. In Genesis 1:28, God gave him dominion over all and in Genesis 2:15-17 He gave him possession of the garden and His only command was not to eat of the tree of knowledge of good and evil.

Adam broke the first covenant given to him by God and as a result man suffered a spiritual death. (Remember Adam's fall because later we will talk about Jesus being declared the second Adam and redeeming us from this curse.) God then made a covenant with Noah. Genesis 9:9 says, "And God spake unto Noah and to his sons with him saying: and I behold I establish my covenant with you, and with your seed after you." As you can see, a covenant is not a new concept to God. God honors his Word. The Bible is an everlasting covenant given to man from God. When you accept Jesus Christ as your Lord and Savior you are automatically a recipient of this covenant. You are given the rights to everything promised by God, but you still have to do your part, which is to be obedient to His will.

Let's look at how God feels about covenant. The basis for God blessing his people lies within Deuteronomy 8:18 which says, "But thou shalt remember the LORD thy God: for it is he that giveth thee power to get wealth, that he may establish his covenant which he sware unto thy fathers, as it is this day." There are many things in this passage of scripture that are noteworthy. The first and foremost lesson from this passage is to never forget your God. Don't forget who allows you to have life and breathe in air daily. Don't forget who pulled you out of the danger and the trouble you have been in. If you want to make God angry, forget what he has done for you. Take a look at Psalm 106 to see what happened when the Israelites forgot what God had done for them in the wilderness. God says that He is the One that gives the power to get wealth. Not your own wit and intellect. Not your smooth tone or good looks. Notice God only gives us the power, it is up to us to get the wealth. God gives you this power for Him not for you. God wants you to live well and look good, but He wants all the glory. Most people get it twisted, it's not about you it's all about Him.

> Ezekiel 20:37 (Amplified) states:
> "And I will cause you to pass under the rod (as the shepherd does his sheep when he counts them, and I will count you as Mine and I will constrain you) and bring you into the covenant to which you are permanently bound."

This is God talking, showing us that the tithe is a covenant matter. It goes much deeper than just us. The King James Version of Ezekiel 20:37 says, "I will bring you into the bond of the covenant." The Greek word for bond is acar. This means God will literally fasten you in and join into battle with you. Glory to God! So the tithe will keep me bound into my covenant with God permanently. God says because of this covenant He will fight with you. Remember, God says He will ever be mindful of His covenant. This means His mind will always be on His covenant. <u>Tithing gives me a right to ask God to fight on my behalf.</u> When you release what's in your hand God will release what's in his hand. You can't afford to hold on to something that does not belong to you. You cannot take the money with you when you die. God sowed Jesus as a firstfruit unto man. For God to move in the heavens you must first move in the earth. You must first release something here so he can release something from above. God requires a natural seed to give a supernatural harvest. Have you ever seen a seed grow that was not sown? God uses the system of sowing and reaping to bless his children. God is not broke and does not need your money. He is the king, and he owns everything. Many people have financial issues because they won't tithe consistently. The devil is after you 24/7, not every other week. So if you are inconsistent with the tithe, God is not obligated to strap you in and scold Satan for you. Inconsistency stems from a lack of faith to believe what God promised in his word. Did you know that faith could be measured? Jesus refers to weak faith, strong faith, and little faith. Weak faith causes you to fall short in bringing the full tithe unto God. Weak faith says, God, I believe you, but I don't know if I trust that you can meet all my needs.

Another term for money is currency. God desires that money flows in your life just as water flows through a hose. However, every time you miss the mark and fail to tithe, it's like bending a water hose, which stops the consistent flow of the water. Another way of looking at it is a cord that has a short circuit. The light continues to flicker on and off. Why? The cord cannot get a consistent current to run through it. The cord is not fully plugged into the source. If you are not tithing you are not fully plugged into the things of God. Going to church is not enough with God to get your needs met. God desires a personal relationship with you, and that means that you will seek to know his will. God will never give a man a hundredfold if he doesn't even understand the first rule pertaining to money, which is God owns everything, and I own nothing. As far back as Genesis, God commanded man to be fruitful and multiply. How can you bear fruit or multiply without first sowing a seed? I cannot get more apple trees without first sowing an apple seed. God told Adam to dress the garden, meaning to cultivate or tend to what He had given Adam. "Be a good steward over my things", is what God is saying. There are many who say the New Testament says to give and not tithe. I have found those to be the same people who will give less than the bare minimum of the ten percent. If you truly believe in giving then you won't mind giving ten percent or more because a true giver understands the money is not theirs anyway. <u>In the kingdom of God, ten percent is the minimum standard that must be met to connect to God's covenant.</u>

The Bible reminds us that God empowers us to establish His covenant. He is referring to the covenant of Abraham. Every truly blessed man and woman has to understand this covenant, because within it lies the wealth of God. The Abrahamic covenant is important because it links us to tithing, and engaging in this covenant will catapult us into a wealthy place. The apostles, prophets, Pharisees, and Sadducees were all aware of their covenant link with Abraham. This is an Old Testament patriarch, but nonetheless, his name was mentioned seventy five times in the New Testament. The book of Acts records an instance of Peter and John referring to Abraham.

Acts 3: 11-13:
And as the lame man which was healed held Peter and John, all the people ran together unto them in the porch that is called Solomon's, greatly wondering. And when Peter saw it, he answered unto the people, "Ye men of Israel, why marvel ye at this? or why look ye so earnestly on us, as though by our own power or holiness we had made this man to walk?" "The God of Abraham, and of Isaac, and of Jacob, the God of our fathers, hath glorified his Son Jesus; whom ye delivered up, and denied him in the presence of Pilate, when he was determined to let him go. "

Notice how he refers to the God of Abraham Isaac and Jacob. Many of the men of the Bible would refer to God in this fashion. Why? God made Abraham promise to pass this covenant down to his children.

Genesis 17: 6-10 states:
And I will make thee exceeding fruitful, and I will make nations of thee, and kings shall come

out of thee. And I will establish my covenant between me and thee and thy seed after thee in their generations for an everlasting covenant, to be a God unto thee, and to thy seed after thee. And I will give unto thee, and to thy seed after thee, the land wherein thou art a stranger, all the land of Canaan, for an everlasting possession; and I will be their God. And God said unto Abraham, "Thou shalt keep my covenant therefore, thou, and thy seed after thee in their generations. "This is my covenant, which ye shall keep, between me and you and thy seed after thee; every man child among you shall be circumcised."

All of the children who were in the lineage of Abraham were taught this covenant. Notice the words that make up this irrevocable promise. God said "I will make you exceedingly fruitful and your only part of the deal is to pass this covenant on to your seed and their generations." This is relevant to our understanding of the covenant. You cannot have God's true wealth and prosperity without understanding this covenant. Can you be rich? Yes, however, I'm talking about completely whole spirit, soul and body. I'm talking about a world changing church, a world changing covenant. Abraham walked with God and God called him His friend and because of their relationship God would not hide anything from him.

Genesis 18: 16-19:
And the men rose up from thence, and looked toward Sodom: and Abraham went with them to bring them on the way. And the LORD said, "Shall I hide from Abraham that thing which I do;" Seeing that Abraham shall surely become a great and mighty nation, and all the nations of the

earth shall be blessed in him? For I know him, that he will command his children and his household after him, and they shall keep the way of the LORD, to do justice and judgment; that the LORD may bring upon Abraham that which he hath spoken of him.

God is waiting on us to take our rightful position on the earth. As the seeds of Abraham, we are supposed to be dominating here on earth. No more church fundraising chicken dinners, no more selling donuts, all we need, is to put into practice the revelation and principles from God's Word. Walking in this revelation is His desire for us, He calls us His friend. We have been walking by sight and not by faith, and that angers God. Abraham was a man of faith; that is why he is called the father of our faith to all who believe in Christ.

Many scholars and theologians argue tithing as a requirement. Unfortunately, they have relied on their natural, earthly way of thinking instead of tapping into the wisdom of an all-knowing God. <u>The tithe is the link to downloading the benefits of the covenant.</u> Adam could "download" from his source in the beginning, who was God. God was the "database," and when Adam fell, he had a spiritual fall, hence, revelation was no longer readily accessible. He could no longer name the animals all over if he had to. Adam disconnected from the original source of all thoughts and wisdom. God being all-wise must have thought that there had to be another way to give it back to my children whom He loved so dearly. So God used Abraham a man of faith, a man who was willing to obey. The first command God gave Abram was to get the out of thy country (Genesis 12) and he obeyed. Ever since that time he never stopped obeying God. God saw Abraham's willingness to obey and chose him as the one;

"I will use him to bless all my future children until Christ comes." That includes you and me.

After Adam's fall, God had to find another man to use in the form of flesh in order to continue to bless man. God works through man. It would be illegal for him to come down to earth in his fullness as a spirit because he gave man dominion. God will never break his own word. That's why Jesus had to come in the form of flesh to take back the keys from Satan. Since God is a Spirit, He gave earth over to mankind to dominate. Man is obligated to bring the likeness of heaven to earth. God is not a man that he should lie. When God spoke that man was to have dominion he literally meant that. That is also why Abraham is so important because he was the vessel God used to put the covenant intact to bless his children after Adam's sin.

<u>It is no accident that Abraham tithed.</u> It is so important that you clearly understand this. The arguments that are made among theologians is that, Abraham didn't understand what he was doing when he tithed. They also claim that tithing wasn't commanded by God, and that Abraham tithed from the spoils of war. This is another attempt at denying the responsibility to tithe as a Christian. Either you believe the word of God, or you don't. What these Biblical scholars attempt to do is find technical loopholes in the Bible. They are in error because they study with the naked eye and not a spiritual eye. To cover the argument that Abraham did not understand what he was doing I encourage you to read John 8:56 where Jesus clearly states, "Your father Abraham rejoiced to see my day: and he saw it, and was glad." I love that scripture. Jesus said that Abraham had revelation of his coming and was rejoicing in heaven when he came because his assignment was not in vain. Glory to God! Abrahams tithing out of "spoils of war" is how the tithe was given. In Abraham's time the tenth was paid out of spoils, produce, or property as they were the primary sources of increase. I'm

not here to have debates, but you must understand the facts and the revelation, or you will easily be talked out of your inheritance and miss God. I can't stand the church looking poor another day and God's people going without while sinners are ruling the earth; all because we fail to tap into one little nugget, the tithe. Tithing is a moral obligation to those who love God not an intent of force.

Is tithing the answer to everything wrong in your life? No, there are other nuggets of truth that will revolutionize your life. Tithing is a biblical principle from God to restore spiritual sight lost in the Garden of Eden. God says in Proverbs 29:18 "Where there is no vision, the people perish." Can you imagine being able to see things before they happen? What would it be like to know what business to open, when to open it and where? What would it be like to have supernatural insight to know where and what to minister; knowing where to go and when? What would it be like to know what investments to make and more importantly, knowing how to hear from your Father in heaven, who has missed talking to you? The Lord desires to give us spiritual insight, but only through our understanding of the details associated with the covenant. We cannot allow the blood of Christ to be shed in vain.

Chapter Three:
THE PURPOSE OF THE TITHE

When you understand the tithe and its relevance to our inheritance in Christ, you have access to sweat less victories. Wouldn't it be nice to let the Lord fight for you? Sweat less victory is just one of the benefits of the tithe. Your tithe will no longer be given out of ignorance. Nor will it be given in vain. Let's take a look at the history of tithing and then look further back into the revelation and the heritage of tithing. Giving you a Biblical understanding will provide some insight as to the purposes of the tithe.

Whenever the purpose of a thing is unknown, abuse is inevitable. So let's discover God's purpose for the tithe. Although Abraham is the believer's link to the tithe, the tithe carried on beyond the law. The tithe is talked about some 38 times in the Bible. Many scholars say the tithe is relevant to the Old Testament only, which is not true. What I have found is that those who look for a way out of tithing are those who don't want to tithe anyway, and any excuse will do when you refuse to be obedient. Those who don't tithe will often say, "I don't tithe, but I know and love God." If you do know Him then why hasn't he spoken to you about being a steward and told you what belongs to Him? Others say, "The Lord understands my situation." Yes, you are absolutely right and

He wants to get you out of that situation, but you must first be obedient.

The first instance of tithing is noted with Abraham, who is the most important link to the tithe. The majority of the remainder of other references to tithing is in the Old Testament when the Lord spoke through Moses. This is the reason most scholars or avid Bible readers say we do not have to tithe, because the Bible tells us we are no longer under the law. It is pertinent to know the customs of the Old Testament so we can get an understanding for the purpose of the tithe. Abraham was not under the law when he tithed, which makes the tithe a fully valid principle today. He tithed actually 430 years prior to the law. The Old Testament provides a valuable foundation for the New Testament revelation. In the book of Leviticus, the patriarch Moses gives instructions to the Israelites from God.

> Leviticus 27:30-34
>
> And all the tithe of the land, whether of the seed of the land, or of the fruit of the tree, is the LORD's: it is holy unto the LORD. And if a man will at all redeem ought of his tithes, he shall add thereto the fifth part thereof. And concerning the tithe of the herd, or of the flock, even of whatsoever passeth under the rod, the tenth shall be holy unto the LORD. He shall not search whether it be good or bad, neither shall he change it: and if he change it at all, then both it and the change thereof shall be holy; it shall not be redeemed. These are the commandments, which the LORD commanded Moses for the children of Israel in Mount Sinai.

The Lord says regardless of where the increase comes from He wants a tenth of all the increase. All the increase means gross. You do not give to God from your net income. He has absolutely nothing to do with Uncle Sam. Render to Ceasar what is his. The tithe is holy. The tithe (tenth) should be separated and set apart from the rest. Leviticus 27 Verse 32 is referring to those times when it was the custom that as the sheep came into the gates of the barn the shepherd would stand and count the sheep in numerical order, one through ten until he got to the tenth. On the tenth sheep he would take his staff marked with color and stamp the tenth sheep as the Lord's.

Now if the tithe was holy in the Old Testament, why wouldn't it be holy in the New Testament? Think about it. The meaning of a thing doesn't change. The meaning of prayer, meditate, jump, hello, goodbye, mop, spray and thank you has not changed in 4000 years so why would the word "holy" change. The actual make up of the tithe is holiness.

If the tithe was holy then, it is still holy now. That means it should be separated from the rest of the lump. Just as the example of the sheep. Mark it. So if the tithe pleased God then why wouldn't it please him now? If he commanded it then why wouldn't it be commanded now? The purpose of the law was to show the people their sin. The purpose of the commandments was to obey God. Notice this was a commandment just as the Ten Commandments. If you call yourself a Christian aren't the commandments of God still valid? Look at Matthew 15:3 when Jesus spoke to the Pharisees.

Matthew 15:2-9

Why do thy disciples transgress the tradition of the elders? for they wash not their hands when they eat bread. But he answered and said unto them, "Why do ye also transgress the commandment of God by your tradition? For God commanded, saying, Honour thy father and mother: and, He that curseth father or mother, let him die the death. But ye say, Whosoever shall say to his father or his mother, It is a gift, by whatsoever thou mightest be profited by me; And honour not his father or his mother, he shall be free. Thus have ye made the commandment of God of none effect by your tradition. Ye hypocrites, well did Esaias prophesy of you, saying, This people draweth nigh unto me with their mouth, and honoureth me with their lips; but their heart is far from me. But in vain they do worship me, teaching for doctrines the commandments of men."

Look at what Jesus said to these biblical teachers. You're trying to focus on one thing when you have not done the commanded things. You cannot focus on giving before paying a tithe. It does not work like that. The tithe has been commanded by God, it is not an option. It is a devoted thing, meaning it is dedicated. In the Old Testament, if a man dedicated anything to God (binding himself with a solemn curse never to alienate it to any other purpose), then it became a devoted thing. That is why the tithe is such a covenant connector with God. He sent word through Moses to command it because the people were not it tune with God. He had to spoon-feed them everything. It wasn't as with Abraham where he walked with God and heard from him. If the Israelites were not told specifically in those days they would have done nothing or continued to live in sin. Notice that Jesus is not trying to put anyone under the law but there are still commands that stand today even after Christ's coming. Look at what Jesus told the rich young ruler.

Matthew 19:16-17:
And, behold, one came and said unto him, Good Master, what good thing shall I do, that I

may have eternal life? And he said unto him, "Why callest thou me good? There is none good but one, that is, God: but if thou wilt enter into life, keep the commandments."

In essence, he was saying, obey God. <u>The tithe is a seed of obedience.</u> By giving the tithe I am saying, I submit my will to God and choose to obey His word. Tithing is an issue of stewardship. God is looking for someone he can trust with seed. The tithe is Gods portion of the seed he requires before a Godly harvest can be released. Adam was called to cultivate the garden. Meaning manage what God gave him. Failure to tithe is a sign of being a poor steward. The beginning of stewardship is first knowing who owns the money and secondly being mature enough to not eat what must be planted.

JOHN 10:15-18:
As the Father knoweth me, even so know I the Father: and I lay down my life for the sheep. And other sheep I have, which are not of this fold: them also I must bring, and they shall hear my voice; and there shall be one fold, and one shepherd. Therefore doth my Father love me, because I lay down my life, that I might take it again. No man taketh it from me, but I lay it down of myself. I have power to lay it down, and I have power to take it again. This commandment have I received of my Father.

As a believer you must be fully persuaded just as Abraham was, not only to live for God but also to obey him. This is Jesus talking to the Jews. Jesus is giving them insight into eternal life and goes on to explain that this was a commandment given to him by God. Notice he tells them that he and his father are one. Even though Jesus was connected directly to the father he still received commandments. That's amazing to me! Commandments are that powerful because they put you in line with God. He said his sheep would know his voice. Do you know the voice of God? If so, why wouldn't you obey his voice? After reading this book you are personally responsible for the information provided in it.

John 14:15:
If ye love me, keep my commandments.

John 14: 21:
He that hath my commandments, and keepeth them, he it is that loveth me: and he that loveth me shall be loved of my Father, and I will love him, and will manifest myself to him.

Your love for God can be based upon the commandments you are willing to keep. He says those who truly love me will have no issues keeping my word. Do you have a problem releasing to God what belongs to him? Many try to argue that commandments automatically put you under the law. Is that true? If so, then why did God command Adam and Eve in the garden? Commands were given in the garden. If it is God's intent to restore us back to the garden where we once dominated and received commands, I would like to make the point that we can receive commands today and still not be under the law.

Numbers 18: 1-24: (Message Bible)
Duties in the Tent of Testimony
God said to Aaron, "You and your sons, along with your father's family, are responsible for taking care of sins having to do with the Sanctuary; you and your sons are also responsible for sins

involving the priesthood. So enlist your brothers of the tribe of Levi to join you and assist you and your sons in your duties in the Tent of Testimony. They will report to you as they go about their duties related to the Tent, but they must not have anything to do with the holy things of the Altar under penalty of death—both they and you will die! They are to work with you in taking care of the Tent of Meeting, whatever work is involved in the Tent. Outsiders are not allowed to help you.

"Your job is to take care of the Sanctuary and the Altar so that there will be no more outbreaks of anger on the People of Israel. I personally have picked your brothers, the Levites, from Israel as a whole. I'm giving them to you as a gift, a gift of God, to help with the work of the Tent of Meeting. But only you and your sons may serve as priests, working around the Altar and inside the curtain. The work of the priesthood is my exclusive gift to you; it cannot be delegated—anyone else who invades the Sanctuary will be executed."

God said to Aaron, "You won't get any inheritance in land, not so much as a small plot of ground: I am your plot of ground, I am your inheritance among the People of Israel."

"I'm giving the Levites all the tithes of Israel as their pay for the work they do in the Tent of Meeting. Starting now, the rest of the People of Israel cannot wander in and out of the Tent of Meeting; they'll be penalized for their sin, and the penalty is death. It's the Levites and only the Levites who are to work in the Tent of Meeting and they are responsible for anything that goes wrong. This is the regular rule for all time. They get no inheritance among the People of Israel; instead

I turn over to them the tithes that the People of Israel present as an offering to God. That's why I give the ruling: They are to receive no land-inheritance among the People of Israel."

Verse 18 gives the basis and purpose of the tithe. The tithes were to be given to the Levite tribe for God to carry out his work. The tithes and offerings were specifically for them to get paid for doing the work of God and to keep the sanctuary for the Jews since they were not allowed to own any land. There were twelve tribes out of Jacob's loins. The and the Levites were chosen to tend to the sanctuary and the high priest (which was Aaron at that time) would offer up these tithes and offerings to God. The term Levitical comes from the term Levite. Jacob had twelve sons and one was named Levi. Levi had three sons (Genesis 46:11). Levi's descendants were selected as the tribe to carry out tabernacle and temple duties. The Levitical priesthood starts with Levi then proceeds through the loins of Aaron. The descendants of Aaron had the privilege of being the actual priests of the temple. The Levites' duties consisted of many things such as: teaching (Leviticus 10:11), judges, they did construction work on the temple, they would translate and they were normally the choir. So they fulfilled many roles and duties normally from age 25 until the age of 50 (Numbers 8:24-50). As you can see the Levite tribe was critical to the success of the early church by carrying out many duties to keep the things of God going forth.

What people fail to understand is that the church lights do not stay on for free. Yes, they actually have a light bill. Some Christians have this poverty mentality where they want a handout, someone to give them something. Something for nothing and give it for free. It is supposed to be through our tithes and offerings that the Church continues to exist and thrive. Satan has deceived many people in this area. He has some people that say they believe in giving ten percent of their income but just not to the church. They want to borrow the principle of the tithe but not give complete credit to the author, God. I personally don't have a problem with the Church having a building fund. It does not matter what you label it, the bottom line is the things of God cannot go forth without money. The problem comes in when so-called Christians don't give like they are supposed to and the Church looks poor. The Church should be the example of excellence and an example of the external image of a good God, not the roof leaking and old pews. That's not God or his will. He desires so much more for his people and his work. Some Christians have been failing to obey God and operate in his principles. We have neglected the command given to us to prosper God's kingdom. Many of us are operating in a failing system that does not work. We are operating in the world's system, which results in destruction. If the church does not catch hold of the biblical truths we are in trouble. As leaders we have to do a better job of teaching people to give. Too many people have the mentality that all the church wants is my money. If you are sitting under bad leadership that is one thing, but when you give your money to the church you are giving unto God not man. We must stop this ignorant mentality of mixing man and God. That comes from a lack of maturity in the things of God. You must develop a deeper relationship with your Heavenly Father so you won't have a problem giving Him what belongs to Him.

 The church overall has been taking a whipping because we have not applied the principles given to us by God so that we may prosper. Tithing is just one of the many principles. Think about it. Doesn't it just make sense to tithe and give an offering so that the Church can continue to minister to God's people? How can the church take care of the poor if the church is poor? I'm not talking about people just mismanaging money. I am referring to the truly poor. For all of you Christians crying about giving to God, if you actually study the Tanakh (Jewish bible) you will actually find that they gave between 23-25% of all their income. The Jewish people were very tithe-conscious. That is why today they are still one of the wealthiest groups of people in the world.

Today we cry about giving anything — not to mention the ten percent we are required to give to God. "Oh, no way I could do that", is what most people say. "What about my bills?" Are you referring to the bills you made on your own or the bills that were created because you purchased items without God's permission? Every person at some point of time in their life has made some poor financial choices. Whether it was a bad purchase or a financial decision that seemed like a good idea at the time, we've all experienced the regret or buyer's remorse. However, giving starts the receiving process; you cannot receive a harvest from a seed that is not sown.

Deuteronomy 14: 22-29 (Message Bible)
Make an offering of ten percent, a tithe, of all the produce which grows in your fields year after year. Bring this into the Presence of God, your God, at the place He designates for worship and there eat the tithe from your grain, wine, and oil and the firstborn from your herds and flocks. In this way you will learn to live in deep reverence before God, you're God, as long as you live. But if the place God, your God, designates for worship is too far away and you can't carry your tithe that far, God, your God, will still bless you: exchange your tithe for money and take the money to the place God, your God, has chosen to be worshiped. Use the money to buy anything you want: cattle, sheep, wine, or beer—anything that looks good to you. You and your family can then feast in

the Presence of God, your God, and have a good time.

Meanwhile, don't forget to take good care of the Levites who live in your towns; they won't get any property or inheritance of their own as you will. At the end of every third year, gather the tithe from all your produce of that year and put it aside in storage. Keep it in reserve for the Levite who won't get any property or inheritance as you will, and for the foreigner, the orphan, and the widow who live in your neighborhood. That way they'll have plenty to eat and God, your God, will bless you in all your work.

The main purpose of the tithe was to present it to God. It was used for the Levites, orphans, widows, foreigners, and poor people. This should also be the primary use for churches today. In today's setting, the Levites would be the church staff including the pastor. II Chronicles gives instructions about making sure that we take care of those who serve the church full-time so that they won't have any distractions or concerns and can give themselves totally to God.

Notice that God said as you bring the tithe it is a form of worship, which allows you to develop a deep reverence for Him. God desires to be worshipped with respect, love, and honor that can only be produced by those who understand and operate in their Covenant rights. <u>Tithing is a form of worship and acknowledging God.</u> There are many churches that don't tithe, but for those of you who do, don't be too fast to judge.

Some churches that tithe have become so religious with the tithe. We have to get out of doing everything the same way every week. We have to let the spirit of God move in his way and his time. We need to move not as we plan it, but as He instructs us. This is the only way God can rain his blessings here in the earth. In the Old Testament God gave specific instructions for bringing the tithe and offerings. God is still speaking today regarding our giving.

God said when you bring your tithe you are worshipping him and a transformation will come about as a result of your worship. Only second to the call for salvation, bringing the tithe should be one of the most important parts of a church service. Why? <u>It allows the people of God to step into the provision of God through their obedience.</u> This moment is pleasing to God and should be equally pleasing for the giver. Those who lack the revelation of the tithe will continue to sit with the same old looks on their faces every Sunday until they began to understand that tithing is not a formality but a personal form of worship to God. The more freedom you give a congregation to worship God in their giving, the more they will give.

It's easier to give to God when you are encouraged to enter into His presence, as opposed to dropping it into a plate or bucket. There are those who always question what is being done with their tax money, but we must also recognize that the same question exist with the tithe. You don't have to wonder when you're releasing the tithe freely in worship while experiencing His presence. It is offensive when we rush the giving of the tithe. This is a critical part of worship that should not be limited because of a failure to recognize the purpose of that moment. We sing, dance, praise, preach and then rush the giving to our most high God. This is important to Him; it's what He has been waiting on. The singing, dancing and preaching are all a form of worship that gives us an opportunity to enter into God's presence, however, we must not forsake our giving to the most high God. God wants an acceptable sacrifice; he wants you to release what belongs to him so he can release what belongs to you! He wants to purify your heart through your giving, but it has to be an environment conducive for giving. The University of Georgia received $108 million dollars in 2006 for donations. Could you imagine if your church received that amount annually in tithes and offerings? What could you do to advance the kingdom of God with that much money? Guess what? Your church should receive that annually.

God is crying out to reveal things to his children. He is yearning to give this revelation to his people. We must give him an opportunity to do so. If your church were taking in $100 million a year, you wouldn't have to have two and three services a day. You could buy a stadium and have one service and take as long as needed to worship Him. I'm trying to stretch your thought process. God is an unlimited God, who has an unlimited bank account. Unlimited means no limits. Take the limits off your imagination. Let God be God. How long will we continue to limit a limitless God? Now is the time to give Him the glory He deserves. It's time we as Christians stop talking about dominating and actually dominate. Let's take a look at what is written in the book of Deuteronomy, chapter 12.

> Deuteronomy 12: 16-18: (Message Bible)
> But you may not eat the blood. Pour the blood out on the ground like water. Nor may you eat there the tithe of your grain, new wine, or olive oil; nor the firstborn of your herds and flocks; nor any of the Vow-Offerings that you vow; nor your Freewill-Offerings and Tribute-Offerings. All these you must eat in the Presence of God, your God, in the place God, your God, chooses—you, your son and daughter, your servant and maid, and the Levite who lives in your neighborhood. You are to celebrate in the Presence of God, your God, all the things you've been able to accomplish.

As we bring our tithes and offerings God wants us to celebrate all the things he has done for us. What god wouldn't show up to be celebrated? What god wouldn't show up to receive what belongs to him? Surely, not the Most High God. Surely, not the God we serve! God says, "Bring the tithe in an atmosphere filled with worship and celebration and I will be there." This is God's desire for the church. As we worship, the high priest (the pastor) is to lift up the tithe and offering to God so that he may find it acceptable and release his vision. Let's look at Deuteronomy 26 in the Message Bible.

Deuteronomy 26: 10-14: (Message Bible)
Then place it in the Presence of God, your God. Prostrate yourselves in the Presence of God, your God. And rejoice! Celebrate all the good things that God, your God, has given you and your family; you and the Levite and the foreigner who lives with you. Every third year, the year of the tithe, give a tenth of your produce to the Levite, the foreigner, the orphan, and the widow so that they may eat their fill in your cities. And then, in the Presence of God, your God, say this:

I have brought the sacred share,
I've given it to the Levite, foreigner, orphan, and widow.
What you commanded, I've done.
I haven't detoured around your commands,
I haven't forgotten a single one.
I haven't eaten from the sacred share while mourning,
I haven't removed any of it while ritually unclean,
I haven't given it to the dead
I haven't used it in funeral feasts.

I have listened obediently to the Voice of God, my God,
I have lived the way you commanded me.

Notice God calls it the sacred share. Are you eating from Gods portion? God wants to know what you will do if times get hard. Will you rob him or will you continue to honor him with your tithe? You will always be tested in the area of finances in your Christian walk and you must master the tithe first. The tithe is required to be sown into good soil if you want to reap a corresponding harvest. No seed can grow if the environment is not conducive for its growth. You cannot sow into bad ground and expect a good harvest

Deuteronomy 26: 15-19: (Message Bible)
Look down from your holy house in Heaven! Bless your people Israel and the ground you gave us, just as you promised our ancestors you would, this land flowing with milk and honey. This very day God, your God, commands you to follow these rules and regulations, to live them out with everything you have in you. You've renewed your vows today that God is your God, that you'll live the way he shows you; do what he tells you in the rules, regulations, and commandments; and listen obediently to him. And today God has reaffirmed that you are dearly held treasure just as he promised, a people entrusted with keeping his commandments, a people set high above all other nations that he's made, high in praise, fame, and honor: you're a people holy to God, your God. That's what he has promised.

This is what you speak to release the blessing over your tithe. God said he will set his people above nations. No more operating on a budget beneath God. No more lack in his house or your house. No more days of going without. Just obey him and he will look down from heaven and pour out a blessing that you won't have room enough to receive.

> Proverbs 3:1-10:
> My son, forget not my law; but let thine heart keep my commandments: For length of days, and long life, and peace, shall they add to thee. Let not mercy and truth forsake thee: bind them about thy neck; write them upon the table of thine heart: So shalt thou find favour and good understanding in the sight of God and man. Trust in the LORD with all thine heart; and lean not unto thine own understanding. In all thy ways acknowledge him, and he shall direct thy paths. Be not wise in thine own eyes: fear the LORD, and depart from evil. It shall be health to thy navel, and marrow to thy bones. Honour the LORD with thy substance, and with the firstfruits of all thine increase:So shall thy barns be filled with plenty, and thy presses shall burst out with new wine.

God is saying don't forget the command of the tithe so that you may have favor. He requires that we acknowledge him. You can acknowledge God by giving unto him. Notice he says that tithing honors him. <u>Paying tithes is a privilege.</u> We should be thankful that God allows us to give back to him what he has so graciously given to us. You don't miss having a driver's license until it's taken from you. I remember my driving instructor telling me that having a license was a privilege. Now I understand exactly what he meant. It's an honor to be able to sit in the presence of the Most High God and lift up to Him our possessions. If more people understood the honor in tithing and the glory it brings God, it would change the church.

Imagine what it would be like to be relieved from struggles. I'm talking about the church and the congregation. This simple principle could unlock that kind of provision from God. Notice He said your barns shall be filled with plenty. In today's times, God is referring to your bank accounts. God said thy presses shall burst out. Something cannot burst until it is full. God says I will fill you up. Close your eyes for a second and think. You know what happens if you shake up a soda and then open it. Imagine that, but imagine it happening to your bank account. You are allowed to partake in the overflow.

Take a moment and meditate on what God tells us in Psalms 50:12-15:

> If I were hungry, I would not tell thee: for the world is mine, and the fullness thereof. Will I eat the flesh of bulls, or drink the blood of goats? Offer unto God thanksgiving; and pay thy vows unto the most High: And call upon me in the day of trouble: I will deliver thee, and thou shalt glorify me.

Everything belongs to God. God says offer up your thanksgiving, your praise, however bring me your vows. Bring me your money. You cannot offer up time in place of the tithe. People say, "I can tithe my time;" no you cannot. The concept of tithing time does not replace the principal of honoring God with your finances. That is not scriptural, nor can you tithe time because that is not part of increase. Remember also in Deuteronomy 14 where he told the children to convert the tithe of livestock and crops into money. God says, "Your making this covenant with me gives you the right to call on me in the day of trouble and I will deliver thee." What a powerful covenant that allows you to call on him, and he promises to deliver.

CHAPTER 4:
THE KEY THAT UNLOCKS

Let's take a look at the most widely used scripture on tithing, the scripture that most believers and non-believers know, Malachi 3.

Malachi 3: 6-12:
For I am the LORD, I change not; therefore ye sons of Jacob are not consumed. Even from the days of your fathers ye are gone away from mine ordinances, and have not kept them. Return unto me, and I will return unto you, saith the LORD of hosts. But ye said, Wherein shall we return? Will a man rob God? Yet ye have robbed me. But ye say, Wherein have we robbed thee? In tithes and offerings. Ye are cursed with a curse: for ye have robbed me, even this whole nation. Bring ye all the tithes into the storehouse, that there may be meat in mine house, and prove me now herewith, saith the LORD of hosts, if I will not open you the windows of heaven, and pour you out a blessing, that there shall not be room enough to receive it.

And I will rebuke the devourer for your sakes, and he shall not destroy the fruits of your ground;

neither shall your vine cast her fruit before the time in the field, saith the LORD of hosts. And all nations shall call you blessed: for ye shall be a delightsome land, saith the LORD of hosts.

Is this scripture still relevant in today's time? Does an apple seed still produce an apple? Remember the purpose of the sun has not changed, neither has the tithe. The outcome of an orange seed planted today, is the same outcome that it had a thousand years ago. There is absolutely nothing wrong with using this scripture to teach on tithing; however, the scripture must be used in it's proper context. This scripture took place at a time when Israel had backslidden from God's commandments.

The Levites stopped the very principles that caused them to blessed. They failed to continue to bring the tithe. So God said, "I will give them another chance, I will send them a messenger." Notice that He says, I will send a messenger of the covenant that you so desire. They wanted the covenant but they were unaware that they already had access to it. The covenant that the Levites were referring to here is the covenant God made with Abraham, Blessed to be a blessing. Malachi 3:6 states, "For I am the LORD, I change not; therefore ye sons of Jacob are not consumed." This is still going on today; People are looking for a pie in the sky, a get rich quick scheme. Still asking, where's my money, just as the Israelites were asking in the scripture, where is my covenant?

The answer to this question is, your covenant is already here! It has already been given to us. God has given us all things pertaining to life and godliness. You are seeking the Lord through things, but where is your obedience? God told the Levites that it was only because of His covenant with Jacob (Abraham's descendant) that He let them live. Remember when God told Abraham to pass the covenant on to every generation? Satan has stepped in and stolen our covenant rights. He has led us to believe that we are supposed to be satisfied with mediocre living. He can't destroy the covenant, but he can try to get us into sin and disobedience just as he did Adam and Eve. So the Lord is saying in Malachi 3, "Return back to the Covenant of the tithe that I made with Abraham."

When you begin to think about it, how can you rob someone of something unless it originally belonged to them? I cannot take your car if you own the title to it. God is saying you robbed me because the tithe was mine from the beginning. God says you are cursed with a curse. Now it's one thing to be cursed, but to be cursed with a curse. Why would such a good God do this? He tells us why. Not only did we disobey Him, but we also robbed Him. Furthermore, he said, "…you robbed the whole nation." God gave us dominion over the earth. This means when God needs to get something done He has to operate through man. So when they stopped tithing, they dishonored God, and as a result the church suffered. So failing to tithe disobeys a commandment and it causes the church to lack.

It is a disgrace when church members do not tithe. This infuriates God and causes him to declare a curse. That is how the work of the kingdom gets done, through tithes and offering. God says not only did you take from me but also the nation suffers because of your disobedience. That's why the body of Christ as a whole is suffering. People don't understand giving to God. That's why he said bring the tithe into the storehouse so there may be meat in his house. There is nothing worse than making the Most High God look poor. It is a disgrace to him. How could we dare make a rich God look so poor? If God called you to start a church he's not going to let you do it in poverty. If you are a pastor you are obligated to preach and teach the truth to the people. This is the only place in the Bible where God says try me and test me. Do you really doubt that He will do as He promised? Notice

God said, "You robbed me in tithes and offering." Keep in mind that I am strictly dealing with the principle of tithe. Please note that the offering is just as important because the offering is the seed that determines your harvest. Now watch what he does in return for your obedience. God is not lacking wisdom since he is the origin of wisdom. He understands that we as his children are encouraged by rewards.

For your obedience of giving the tithe, he says he will open up the windows of heaven and pour us out a blessing. You better praise him! You have got to get this. He says, "Because you have obeyed I will open up the windows of heaven. This is the reward for all the days that you have been tithing, all the years." God says, "I will open the gates." That means it was shut or locked before if he had to open it. So your tithe is a key, a key to God's treasure chest that unlocks vision. If you have not been tithing and you want to start obeying, say hello to VISION. The opening of the window signifies vision, the ability to see. Not with your natural eyes but with your spiritual eyes. No more deception. No more lies and deceit. I can now have access just as Abraham and Adam did before he sinned when he downloaded directly from God. Oh, how wonderful is His name! I don't have to struggle anymore. I can download from my Heavenly Father. I can see where to go and what to do. I once was blind but now I see. I no longer have to suffer from the ignorance of what's been hindering my progress as well as the church's progress.

Proverbs 29:18 states, where there is no vision, the people perish: but he that keepeth the law, happy is he. The church no longer has to suffer. Being a consistent tither offers you insight into the future and allows you to download revelation directly from God. Where there is no vision the people perish but where there is vision the people prosper. Once you know your rights you have to place a demand on this promise of vision from God. He did not have to allow us to present the tithe to him. God doesn't need our little ten percent. You have to go before God and place a demand on your seed by saying "God I have done as you have commanded of me. I have given unto you what is rightfully yours. I command that the window of heaven open now and release vision unto me, so that I may advance your work here on earth God."

If you place a demand on your tithe, God will begin to speak to his people loud and clear once again as he did with our forefathers. Every member of the church is supposed to be prosperous. Our churches should be flooded with millionaires. The power of the tithe is this: It gives access to INSIGHT, WISDOM, and WITTY IDEAS. Christians are supposed to be the cream of the crop in everything they touch, EVERYTHING. Why? Why wouldn't you be if you have tapped into the father of all good things and good ideas? Christians should find the cure for AIDS, cancer and every other foul disease that Satan has imposed on our earth. This earth belongs to us, but we can't take it over without revelation. The tithe gives us back what was stolen in the Garden of Eden. Satan couldn't completely take our vision, so he attempted to sidetrack us to prevent us from walking in the benefits of tithing.

We have been tithing out of tradition and religion without revelation of the rewards of tithing. Please don't let this slip away from you. You no longer have to give your tithe and not receive anything back. The tithe's purpose with the help of the Holy Spirit is to guide you into the right place to reap your harvest. Without vision you will never reach your full potential. Vision drives you when no one else is around. It will push you when no one is looking. Vision is the voice that tells ideas, I can make you come to pass. Pursuing a God-given vision attracts the provision of God. If God gives you a vision he will be present to help you make it come to pass as long as you use your faith.

Vision is the supernatural ability to see into the future based on internal prophesies from God, the downloading of the supernatural for ten cents of every dollar. I'm not saying God is selling himself or selling vision. I am saying there are rewards for obeying God. There are rewards for tithing. If you are not tithing don't let a dime rob you of your vision. Don't let ten cents limit your future. Ten cents out of every dollar gives you vision. Would you rather continue to see things through your eyes or the eyes of God? Look at the vision Daniel had. He fasted and prayed but he was also a devout Jew. I believe that many of the prophets of the Old Testament tithed. It was part of the commandment of the blessing. If they didn't, I believe God would have come and rebuked them just as he did the Levites for robbing him. Ever since I got a hold of this revelation, the Lord has been moving in a great way in my life. I have been placing a demand on vision from God. The Lord has been showing me things that I have never seen before. Just the other day I was talking with a man on the phone and the Lord spoke to me and gave me his exact location, the store name and his whereabouts. The information was 100 % correct. This just totally overwhelmed me. Visions have been dropping into my spirit, and it's wonderful. I can't wait to see what he is going to do next.

Look at Jacob's life as a tither. His grandfather Abraham tithed and taught his grandson. Genesis 28:22 says, "And of all that thou shalt give me I will surely give the tenth unto thee." He said, "I promise to give God what belongs to Him." Isaac (his father) had just finished praying the blessing of Abraham over Him, so he understood the power of the tithe. He used his obedience of the tithe to tap into vision to make him rich. Jacob had worked a hard toiling fourteen years for Laban. He worked for him seeking Rachel's (Leah's sister) hand in marriage. What he didn't know is that Laban was a trickster. After seven years of sweat Laban gave him his first daughter's (Leah) hand in marriage, instead of Rachel whom he loved.

Jacob had become a man of integrity, which he was not always. So he worked another seven years for Rachel's hand. Laban was an old scoundrel. He paid Jacob a slave's hire, which wouldn't even equate to minimum wage in today's time. After serving his last tenure for the love of his life Jacob went to Laban requesting departure with his new family. Laban knew the power of Jacob's God because of the increase that came upon his own house. The fact that you are anointed and have favor should not be a secret. Kenneth Copeland cannot hide his anointing neither can Creflo Dollar because they wear it as if it were a cloak. People should know that you know God not just because you say it but also because everything around you prospers. Jesus cursed the branch that did not bear fruit. We are commanded to multiply. Multiplying only comes through an understanding of your covenant rights. Jacob understood his covenant, his ability to tap into the vision of God. Laban realized the blessing on his life and pleaded with him to stay.

Genesis 30: 32-38:
Let me pass through all your flock today, removing from it every speckled and spotted animal and every black one among the sheep, and the spotted and speckled among the goats; and such shall be my wages.

So later when the matter of my wages is brought before you, my fair dealing will be evident and answer for me. Every one that is not speckled and spotted among the goats and black among the sheep, if found with me, shall be counted as stolen.

And Laban said, "Good; let it be done as you say."

But that same day [Laban] removed the he-goats that were streaked and spotted and all the she-goats that were speckled and spotted, every one that had white on it, and every black lamb, and put them in charge of his sons.

And he set [a distance of] three days' journey between himself and Jacob; and Jacob was then left in care of the rest of Laban's flock.

But Jacob took fresh rods of poplar and almond and plane trees and peeled white streaks in them, exposing the white in the rods.

Then he set the rods which he had peeled in front of the flocks in the watering troughs where the flocks came to drink. And since they bred and conceived when they came to drink.

GENESIS 31: 10-11:

And it came to pass at the time that the cattle conceived, that I lifted up mine eyes, and saw in a dream, and, behold, the rams which leaped upon the cattle were ringstraked, speckled, and grisled.

And the angel of God spake unto me in a dream, saying, Jacob: And I said, Here am I.

Jacob let Laban know he had nothing before he arrived. Laban had a measly, lame flock prior to Jacob turning them into a multitude. The anointing on Jacob's life made Laban's household rich. Laban realized this and asked Jacob what he wanted from him so that he would stay, Jacob responded to Laban just as his grandfather Abraham responded to Melchizedek. Jacob told Laban that he refused to allow any man to make him rich only God. What Jacob meant was, he didn't need any handouts, since he had the Spirit of God dwelling inside of him and the vision of God to guide him.

Jacob was a patient man. He was never worried about money. If so he would never have worked for the measly wages that Laban paid him. He worked for the love of his life and turned down money for the love of God. He loved Rachel so much that he practically worked for free. He loved God and knew God was his source, not Laban, so Jacob was adamant about Laban keeping what he had. Jacob felt like he had something greater on the inside, something more powerful to guide him. Jacobs's grandfather had already told him, <u>you don't need money you need vision.</u> So he tithed when times were hard for fourteen years. He tithed when it wasn't convenient, when he didn't feel like it. You can do that when you know. Know what? That <u>God is your source,</u> even when times get hard. God is my source. Even when the odds seem to be against me, God is my source. Even when it looks tough in the natural, the blood of Christ seals my covenant. I can do all things through Christ who strengthens me. When the image of your "tithe covenant" gets in your heart you can stand boldly and say no devil in hell can stop what my God has for me!! I've got too much vision to pretend I'm blind. Too much wisdom to say I'm broke. To much Christ to pretend it's over. I have a blood-bought covenant that seals my victory. Hallelujah! Help is not on the way it has already come. His name is Jesus Christ.

Now, notice what Jacob did. He said, "Give me the speckled, spotted, and the dark lambs. I will take the ones that are unclean and have issues so you won't say I tried to cheat you as you have done me. I will show you how great my God is. So Laban granted his wish. Laban was scared of someone deceiving him because that's how he dealt with Jacob. So his solution was to take his flock three days away from Jacob's new flock. Jacob had heard from God and believed Him. As Jacob's flock would go down to the troughs to drink water he would take rods and pile strakes in them, a God given ingenious idea. The cattle would them produce just as he had envisioned.

Carrying the seed of the tithe is critical to your success. The Bible says the cattle conceived. Before something birthed in the cattle in the natural realm something first had to be sown by Jacob in the supernatural. Remember when we talked about how Satan tricks Christians through misconception? He has tried for a long time to get Christians to abort the tithe. That's why so many today don't tithe. <u>Satan knows that if he can get you to eat, release, or neglect the seed you will go without vision.</u>

Satan tried to tell my mother that I would never exist. The doctor told my mother that she would never have children. Can you imagine the emotional stress of believing that you could never bear a child or even a vision? You must understand the potency of the tithe. It is like carrying a child for nine months. For the woman to get pregnant the sperm must meet the female ovum or egg before conception can take place. (This is the same concept that applies to your tithe. If Satan can stop you from getting the revelation of tithing then he can stop conception of the vision. You don't know which tithe will break loose the vision needed to seal your future. That is why it must be brought constantly from all increase). A man produces sperm constantly and there are things that could affect his ability to produce. That is why the doctor will tell you that a healthy lifestyle and diet will help the strength of the sperm. Tithing but living like a heathen will affect your ability to receive this gift from God. Just because you have sperm doesn't mean it's reaching the egg. Just because you're tithing doesn't mean it's reaching the throne room. Are you tithing and still shacking up? Are you tithing and still committing adultery? Are you tithing and still have hatred against your brother? Is your heart right when you tithe? Are you murmuring and complaining about tithing? Are you totally convinced why you tithe? Are you a cheerful giver or does it burden you to release money? All these things are conducive to creating the right environment for the tithe to go forth.

A female is born with all the eggs that she will ever have. God already has the provision you need, but it must be met with the tithe. No sperm, no egg fertilization, no baby. No tithe, no key to unlock the window for vision. For a woman to get pregnant all the conditions have to be biologically right. In our case, God is already pregnant but you must create the proper environment for him to give you a baby. The word in itself is pregnant. If you create the wrong environment with the wrong words you will abort the baby. You can't walk around talking broke and think a baby is going to be birthed. It will never happen. The tithe is the key that unlocks the window, but the word is the sperm. You must learn what God has to say about your financial situation so that the baby will not be aborted. Every time you say negative and false reports you kill the vision of God for your life. Don't forget that prior to conception there is preconception. Things you can do to try to make sure your body is ready to carry the baby. During this period God is making sure you are in place before the conception takes place. Are you praying regularly? Do you fast? Are you walking in love? All these things are important to making sure that things on your end are properly set for the baby. Once pregnant, you must care for the baby in the womb. Once God gives you the vision you must feed it and nurture it so that it will continue to grow until birth. Studies show that during pregnancy a women's eye condition may change until she actually gives birth. Upon receiving vision from God you have to begin to see things differently. You cannot continue to look at things in the same light as before. Doing this will stunt your growth tremendously. You must now begin to see things the way that God sees them. With God the only way you can fail to conceive vision is one of two ways. The first way is not tithing at all. Not tithing is like not even having intercourse. There is no sperm available to even conceive the child. The second way is being pregnant and without knowing it. There is nothing harder than tithing and not knowing that you have a right to be pregnant with vision. Tithing gives you the access to vision. You can take that to the bank and cash it, God's bank account that is.

The Bible says Jacob increased exceedingly. How did Jacob increase like this? He had a dream, a vision. What caused this to happen? The tithe released unto him the very same thing it released unto his grandfather Abraham, vision. Just as God gave Abraham sight to see 400 years into his future (Genesis 15:31) he gave Jacob the vision he needed to go forth and prosper. This revelation of vision came to Jacob in Genesis 28. His father Isaac had prayed the blessing of Abraham over him. This is a powerful blessing because it empowers you to prosper. The Bible says Jacob went away to Padanaram, upon his journey he fell into a deep sleep and had a vision. The Lord came to him and promised to give him the land and through him all the families of the earth would be blessed. God was trying to carry out the covenant He had made with Abraham. Consider Jacob's response as he woke up:

> Genesis 28:16-22:
> And Jacob awaked out of his sleep, and he said, "Surely the LORD is in this place; and I knew it not."
> And he was afraid, and said, "How dreadful is this place! this is none other but the house of God, and this is the gate of heaven."
> And Jacob rose up early in the morning, and took the stone that he had put for his pillows, and set it up for a pillar, and poured oil upon the top of it.

And he called the name of that place Bethel: but the name of that city was called Luz at the first.

And Jacob vowed a vow, saying, "If God will be with me, and will keep me in this way that I go, and will give me bread to eat, and raiment to put on, So that I come again to my father's house in peace; then shall the LORD be my God: And this stone, which I have set for a pillar, shall be God's house: and of all that thou shalt give me I will surely give the tenth unto thee."

Jacob said this is too good to be true. The presence of the Lord had engulfed his very being. Jacob finally realized that the dreams and visions he received were from the Lord. Jacob proclaimed this is the house of the Lord. The dream overpowered his very being so much that he made a vow unto God. In those days vows would not be made unto God unless you could carry them out. Vows were as serious as unto death. He said. "I'm so sure about this tithe that I will surely give a tenth for the rest of my days unto you." Jacob caught the revelation of the tithe just as his grandfather and father had told him. He finally got it! The tithe releases vision!" That's why Joseph was such a dreamer. Jacob passed on the covenant revelation of the tithe. That is why Joseph had insight far beyond his natural mind. The covenant of the tithe was being passed down and the visions became stronger through the generations!

CHAPTER 5:
WHY TITHE?

Dreams are the seeds of vision. Many of the greatest ideas and inventions were given to men in dreams. God said, "If you can envision it, I will give it to you." Envision, meaning to see inwardly. God says if you can get it in your spirit when He begins to show it to you, you can have it. Vision pulls you in the direction of your destiny. Vision pushes you out to sea from shallow to deep water. Vision gives you energy when times are hard. Let's look at Webster's definitions of vision:

    1 a : something seen in a dream, trance, or ecstasy; especially : a supernatural appearance that conveys a revelation b : a thought, concept, or object formed by the imagination c : a manifestation to the senses of something immaterial 2 a : the act or power of imagination b (1) : mode of seeing or conceiving (2) : unusual discernment or foresight <a person of vision> c : direct mystical awareness of the supernatural usually in visible form 3 a : the act or power of seeing : SIGHT b : the special sense by which the qualities of an object (as color, luminosity, shape, and size) constituting its appearance are perceived through a process in which light rays entering

the eye are transformed by the retina into electrical signals that are transmitted to the brain via the optic nerve 4 a : something seen b : a lovely or charming sight

In the Bible, God would often speak to man through dreams. My favorite definition is: a supernatural appearance that conveys a revelation. That is what the tithe does. It allows you to tap into supernatural revelation from a higher power. If you are a Christian you walk by faith and not by sight. It should be something moving and stirring your inner being and directing your inner being. Tithing should increase your faith for the things of God. Vision allows the impossible to become possible. Have you ever done something that nobody thought you could do? I guarantee you that at some point in time you envisioned yourself doing it. You saw yourself engaging in it, living it. God desires for all his children to have this kind of vision and insight. No longer should we as Christians suffer behind the eight ball of the world's system, always on the tail end of every major breakthrough. The only way to create our own heaven on earth is to tap into the Kingdom of God's system, and to believe that we can do all things through Christ who gives us strength.

10 Reasons to Tithe

Let's finish breaking down God's words through his prophet Malachi. God said if I would tithe he would bless me, but that should not be my motivation for tithing. So why should I tithe? Here are ten answers to this question:

1. I want to obey God. Tithing is a command from God that he never released us from. It still stands today. If I want to build a relationship with my father I must first start with obeying him. I want to obey him because I love him, not just for provision. However, obedience is the key to provision. Deuteronomy 28 tells me that if I obey God that the blessings of the Lord will overtake me! God

says, "If you obey me I will suddenly overpower you." He says the blessing will come on you. Notice obedience causes God to empower you to prosper.

2. I trust God and I want him to trust me. Tithing is a trust factor. God says, "If I can't trust you with 10% I know I can't trust you with 100%." God wants to bless us beyond our wildest dreams but he must first know he can trust us.

3. In releasing your tithe you are saying, "God I am making you my only source. I don't want any man to say he made me rich." That's what Abraham said and you can do the same. By giving the tithe you are saying, "I want to do things your way God and I understand that you are my provider." I understand that every step towards self-sufficiency is a step away from God.

4. Giving your tithe says, "I want to submit my will to God." Releasing the tithe says, "God your will and not mine." It is the ultimate form of submission and an acceptable form of giving unto the Lord. When your will aligns with the will of God the result will be abundance.

5. It honors God and he is pleased when we bring forth the tithe. God is happy that we show reverence to him, as we should. Tithing shows a deep respect for God and shows him that we choose him as our master and not mammon.

6. I want to see the work of God go forth. I understand that tithing is God's system for getting his work done here on earth. Without the tithe the church would not be as prosperous, therefore making our God look as though he is poor.

7. The tithe doesn't belong to me; I am a steward over God's things. God owns 100% of my income. My job is to distribute the money as he instructs me.

8. Tithing puts me in covenant with God. I understand that God is a covenant God and tithing is a form

of covenant. Abraham made a covenant with God and I am Abraham's seed. Therefore, I can take part in the covenant.

9. I want to be governed by the word of God. I want to live my life according to the word of God, which is his will. I also believe that tithing is His will based upon His word.

10. I believe that in exchange for be obedient to tithing God releases his vision for my life. I must release my faith for the gift of vision and place a demand on God's word for it.

However, when you do not tithe, you are making a statement. To deny tithing is to deny that God exists. <u>When you deny tithing you deny the hand of God, the provision of God and the vision of God.</u> You deny the hand of God because He promised He would rebuke the devourer for your sake. That means, He will protect me from Satan that I might bear fruit that is pleasing to Him. Remember, Satan roams about as a roaring lion seeking whom he may devour. Satan is looking for someone who is not in covenant with God that he may devour. I hope you just caught that revelation. God says if you are a tither He will rebuke Satan so that he may not destroy your harvest. God says you are in covenant and He won't allow anyone to touch your fruit. Then God says nations shall call you blessed. Why? They can see you are in covenant with the Most High God. Satan should not be the number one struggle for Christians. He has already been defeated. God rebukes Satan so you can see where the next harvest is located. To deny tithing says, "God I don't trust you as my source and I don't need your provision. I believe I can do better on my own. I can be whole without your covering." Are you bold enough to make this statement to God?

Lastly, to deny tithing is to say you don't need vision from God. You are saying you don't need to see ahead. I don't need to see the pitfalls that can be avoided. I don't need to accomplish anything big in my life. I don't need you to open up that window so I can see. I choose to remain blind. I hope you are getting this. There are a couple of things God is telling us in Malachi. He is saying, "I am the king, I own the land, and I will protect you." He lets us know that he is our covering. God says if you release to Me what's Mine already I will give you insight. You no longer have to catch the deals when they're gone, always finding out about the million-dollar deal after it's done. Tithing will allow you to see the future just as Abraham has. I recently rode into a town that I had previously tried to put a real-estate deal together three years prior. My deal fell through and at that time I was told I could not build a house on this particular piece of land because the lot was to narrow. Needless to say three years later someone else had built a new house on the land. My lack of vision cost me a great deal of money. I refuse to go any longer without having supernatural insight in my life.

Jacob was tapped into this awesome power and principle of God that he learned from his grandfather Abraham. Let's look at our father of faith, Abraham. He was the first man to ever tithe. This was no accident by any stretch of the imagination. Remember, he was a prophet and a man of God. God said he walked with him continually and habitually and had a strong, consistent ongoing relationship, no gaps in between. God said in Genesis 18, "Shall I hide from Abraham that thing which I do;" and he said it not as a question but as a statement.

Just as God said He would not withhold anything from Abraham, that would also include the revelation of the tithe. The argument by some theologians is that Abraham didn't really know what he was doing when he tithed. (That qualifies as one of the dumbest things that I have ever heard!).

Abraham was willing to sacrifice his son to God because of his love and obedience. The giving of his son represented an Old Testament foreshadow of the coming of Christ and God offering Christ as a sacrifice. Many Christians believe that tithing is only valid for the Old Testament, and that we are New Testament believers. We are New Testament believers, but the Old Testament should not be disregarded. That's why Abraham tithed 430 years before the law even came into place. He was never under the law; it was pure downloading just as Adam did when he named the animals.

Galatians 3:29
And if ye be Christ's, then are ye Abraham's seed, and heirs according to the promise.

If you are a born again believer then you are a seed of Abraham and you have a right to the same covenant God gave him. Pay close attention to how this man of God tithed.

Genesis 14:18-23
And Melchizedek king of Salem brought forth bread and wine: and he was the priest of the most high God.
And he blessed him, and said, "Blessed be Abram of the most high God, possessor of heaven and earth:
And blessed be the most high God, which hath delivered thine enemies into thy hand. And he gave him tithes of all."
And the king of Sodom said unto Abram, "Give me the persons, and take the goods to thyself."
And Abram said to the king of Sodom, "I have lift up mine hand unto the LORD, the most high God, the possessor of heaven and earth,

That I will not take from a thread even to a shoelatchet, and that I will not take any thing that is thine, lest thou shouldest say, I have made Abram rich."

This a portion of the scripture is when Lot, Abraham's nephew, had gotten in trouble. He was captured by an army of bandits, then Abraham had to rescue him. The Scriptures resume after this rescue.

GENESIS 14: 16-23:
And he brought back all the goods, and also brought again his brother Lot, and his goods, and the women also, and the people.
And the king of Sodom went out to meet him after his return from the slaughter of Chedorlaomer, and of the kings that were with him, at the valley of Shaveh, which is the king's dale.
And Melchizedek king of Salem brought forth bread and wine: and he was the priest of the most high God.
And he blessed him, and said, Blessed be Abram of the most high God, possessor of heaven and earth:
And blessed be the most high God, which hath delivered thine enemies into thy hand. And he gave him tithes of all.
And the king of Sodom said unto Abram, Give me the persons, and take the goods to thyself.
And Abram said to the king of Sodom, I have lift up mine hand unto the LORD, the most high God, the possessor of heaven and earth,
That I will not take from a thread even to a shoelatchet, and that I will not take any thing

that is thine, lest thou shouldest say, I have made Abram rich:

There are many things we need to notice here. This passage of scripture will lead us to the New Testament. The first thing to notice is that Melchizedek brought forth bread and wine. Does that sound like anything you've ever heard of? How about communion? This is the foreshadowing of Christ's coming and the passing of the covenant from Melchizedek to Christ. Communion is a joyous act of thanksgiving for all God has done, is doing, and will do. Communion is the most intimate experience of fellowship in the presence of God. Abraham and Melchizedek partook of communion to honor the coming of someone much greater than both of them. Communion means to be transformed. When Abraham was 75 years old, God prophesied to him that he would be the father of many nations. When God speaks something, it is already done in the eyes of God. It just took Abraham some time to walk in this revelation from God. God did not change Abraham's name from Abram until he tithed and received vision from God. His name was changed to Abraham 15 years later after walking out this vision. Abraham's greatest blessings did not manifest until after he tithed. All this happened 430 years before the law even existed. This is important because Romans 6:14 says, "Ye are not under the law, but under grace."

This is the argument that scholars try to make in an attempt to stop people from tithing. They say we are to give only under the new covenant. A covenant-minded Christian would have no problem giving ten percent. In fact, a covenant minded Christian would give much more than ten percent. When you begin to operate in the blessing of the tithe and walk in overflow you do not have to be limited to only ten percent. When you understand that you own nothing and God owns everything that should cause you to give when God instructs you to. This kind of giving is overflow giving and will always result in more than ten percent. I find that the majority that try to finagle their way out of the ten percent and try to use the argument of giving in place of tithing usually don't even give ten percent of their income but would much rather talk someone else out of their blessing. The argument as to whether or not Abraham knew what he was doing when he tithed to Melchizedek wouldn't exist, if one truly understood the walk he had with God. God clearly gave him insight into the future so that we may all be blessed. That is why God told him that this covenant and blessing would last a thousand generations. A thousand generations has still not passed.

John 8:56 says, "Your father Abraham rejoiced to see my day: and he saw it, and was glad." This is Jesus talking which clearly lets us know that God gave Abraham a vision of the coming of Jesus Christ. So he knew that the tithe was our covenant connection to Christ. God would not have promised Abraham such a blessing and not give him the wisdom to keep the blessing alive and active for the thousand generations. The tithe keeps the covenant alive, and tithing is a principle that went beyond the cross. Most things in the Old Testament died at the cross when Jesus went under. Most things accept the tithe. The tithe went beyond the cross and still lives today.

Let's look at why tithing is still valid today. Besides Hebrews, there are only four verses that discuss Melchizedek. The other verses are in Genesis 14 when Abraham gave him the tithes. I have already explained the importance of our connection with Abraham as believers. Our material blessing is linked through him based on the covenant he made with God. Melchizedek is the torch passer of the tithe covenant in the spiritual realm, a type of Christ. Abraham is the initiator of this in the natural.

Hebrews 6:20

Whither the forerunner is for us entered, even Jesus, made an high priest for ever after the order of Melchizedek.

Notice that God says Christ is a priest eternally and after the order of Melchizedek. The word order translated in Hebrew is ordained, appointed, or in fixed succession. This means God preordained Christ or put Him in place to pick up where Melchizedek left off, to receive the tithe.

Hebrews 7:1-4

For this, Melchizedek, king of Salem, priest of the most high God, who met Abraham returning from the slaughter of the kings, and blessed him;

To whom also Abraham gave a tenth part of all; first being by interpretation King of righteousness, and after that also King of Salem, which is, King of peace;

Without father, without mother, without descent, having neither beginning of days, nor end of life; but made like unto the Son of God; abideth a priest continually.

Now consider how great this man was, unto whom even the patriarch Abraham gave the tenth of the spoils.

Hebrews 7:17-28

For he testifieth, Thou art a priest for ever after the order of Melchizedek.

For there is verily a disannulling of the commandment going before for the weakness and unprofitableness thereof.

For the law made nothing perfect, but the bringing in of a better hope did; by the which we draw nigh unto God. And inasmuch as not without an oath he was made priest:

(For those priests were made without an oath; but this with an oath by him that said unto him, The Lord sware and will not repent, Thou art a priest for ever after the order of Melchizedek:)

By so much was Jesus made a surety of a better testament.

And they truly were many priests, because they were not suffered to continue by reason of death:

But this man, because he continueth ever, hath an unchangeable priesthood.

Wherefore he is able also to save them to the uttermost that come unto God by him, seeing he ever liveth to make intercession for them.

For such an high priest became us, who is holy, harmless, undefiled, separate from sinners, and made higher than the heavens;

Who needeth not daily, as those high priests, to offer up sacrifice, first for his own sins, and then for the people's: for this he did once, when he offered up himself.

For the law maketh men high priests which have infirmity; but the word of the oath, which was since the law, maketh the Son, who is consecrated for evermore

This passage of scripture kills any debate of whether to tithe or not. This scripture clearly states that Jesus took the reign of Melchizedek, who was a type of Christ until Jesus came. He had the position of an earthly king and a heavenly priest. Melchizedek's name stood for peace and righteousness.

God says his reign is continual or perpetual, meaning ongoing. His reign does not stop. It never stopped until Jesus came and took over his position. Jesus fulfilled the order of Melchizedek. Many say that the New Testament does not talk about tithing but it is spoken of eight times in this chapter alone.

God says in Hebrews 7:4, "Consider how great his ways..." which means pay attention to who this man is. Some may say the New Testament does not talk about tithing. Yes, it does. We just read the scriptural connection of Melchizedek. If you read Hebrews, Paul had just finishing teaching them how to be more mature Christians before explaining to them Jesus fulfilling Melchizedek's priesthood. It was never God's intention that we live the rest of our lives giving animal sacrifices. He knows the beginning and the end. God is all knowing. He set Melchizedek up as high priest. The Latin word for priest is "pontifex" which means bridge builder. Melchizedek was set up to be a bridge builder for Christ's return. Melchizedek's reign was everlasting which means tithing never stopped. So tithing is just as valid today as it was 2000 years ago. This is a key to your success to begin operating in the kingdom of God's system.

After reading this book you should be fully equipped to see spiritually, with no more scales or setbacks. Get ready for momentum overflow. It is imperative, that with this new revelation of tithing you will have to stay away from negative people and comments. The devil will do all he can to steal the Word from you. Satan knows that tithing is much bigger than one individual. Ten percent of one individual's income cannot change the world. However, ten percent of everyone's income can. That is why Satan attacks the church and Christians in the area of finances. Satan desires the church to look poor, and to keep scandals surfaced, so that the image of the church can be destroyed. For years, many have failed to take the church seriously because the church as a whole has been lacking, in comparison to what the world has to offer. If your God is so great why doesn't the church have air conditioning? This is a question Satan has some people asking.

The church has to take its vision to another level, so that the wealth of God can be restored to his people. Once this restoration takes place, God can be glorified and the power of the earth taken back and put in its rightful place. No more sad stories to discredit a good God. I have heard it all. I have counseled people about their finances and asked them if they tithe. I have heard thousands of stories. One man told me someone lost their house because they tithed. Or someone filed bankruptcy because of tithing. All of the outcomes may be true but the origin of the problem was not tithing. Giving God 10 percent out of a 100 percent has never sent anyone down the tubes, but poor stewardship has. Tithing was never designed to make you poorer than before. It's amazing how 10 percent can test the heart, mind and will, when tithing is truly a privilege. If only more Christians looked at tithing as gaining something instead of losing something. Christians need to realize that God rewards obedience. The reality is that God's system was not designed that way. Christians are supposed to walk by faith and not by sight. Just as faith is designed to please Him, so is obedience. Your obedience is designed to release vision. Whether you decide to tithe or not, the tithe still belongs to God.

Anyone who neglects tithing after reading this book, has determined in their minds, that they are not going to tithe. God is an orderly God. If you cannot pass the test to tithe, you are not going to connect with God's vision. You have chosen money, over God, to be your master. The 10 percent is just a test for you, to see in whom you put your trust. Who do you want to be your own source? Is the will of your mind greater than a desire to love God who sent his only son to die for you? Tithing is a simple test that many do not pass. You may say, I am a single parent and barely make enough to pay bills. How do you expect me to give 10 percent when I can barley keep my lights on? My answer to you would be, you cannot afford not to give God the tenth if you are struggling financially. You may be in the jam that you are in, because you don't have a vision. You need to tithe so God can help you to see your way out of the mess that you are in. He also promised that he would keep Satan off your harvest. The tithe is so important and critical for your success.

CHAPTER 6:
THE BOY WHO BELIEVED IN THE TITHE

"Mommy, can we go to church tomorrow?"

That was Andre's battle cry every Saturday at 5:30 p.m., after his mom made him come in, from playing basketball. He was only ten years old, but could outplay the fifteen-year olds that he would play with. He was naturally talented, but that wasn't his passion. His true passion was church. Basketball was just an outlet, since he lived in the one of the worst projects this side of town. There was nothing else for him to do. All of his other siblings were older. Two of his older brothers were locked up, one was dead, and a sister he had never seen. That was the extent of little Andre's life - basketball and church. How he would live for Sunday. I saw him in the sanctuary one day and watched him praising away. For goodness sakes, half the grownups weren't even praising

TEN CENTS TO PROSPER

Him. Immediately I knew that this little boy was called to the ministry. He would flail his arms to the sky as if he just knew that his God loved him as much as he did his God. He was a special kid. I began to notice that he never went to children's

church. It was as if he didn't belong there. He knew that the sanctuary was his place of worship. I remember that very day when he came down the church hallway in his ripped suit pants. I stopped him and asked him his name. "Andre," he proclaimed as he glanced around me to continue."

"What do you want to be when you grow up, Andre?"

"A preacher, sir."

Chills ran down my spine. To have heard a child say that, it does something to me every time I think about it. After noticing his clothing, I reached into my pocket to slide out fifty bucks. He then asked, "Did you hear Dr. Johnson preach today?"

I chuckled inside and said; "Yes, I did, Andre, did you?"

"Yes!" he proclaimed. "Dr. Johnson said when we give to God it pleases Him."

"You are absolutely correct." I responded, "It all belongs to Him, Andre. He just requires our obedience."

"You mean obey sir."

"Exactly Andre."

As I quietly slid the fifty dollar bill out, thoughts of new pants for Andre came into my mind. Little did I know God had something else in mind.

That fifty dollar "seed" was a seed of inspiration for a boy who was called for greatness. Andre held that money until the following Sunday. When it came time for the offering basket to pass by, Andre raised his hand for a tithe envelope. His mom pushed his hand back down quickly, since all she ever put in the basket was three dollars maximum on her best Sunday. But Andre raised his hand again. Miss Betsy smacked him harder and asked him what he was doing. He

said, "Mom, I've got to pay my tithes." "You don't have any money boy, put your hand down
before I whip you."

"But mom, I do!"

"Where is the money?"

He proceeded to pull the fifty dollars out of his torn left sock. His mom's eyes grew wide and before she could get the words out, he told her that one of the ministers gave it to him last week. As she went to jerk the money from him he turned his shoulder quickly as if he was on the basketball court shielding his ball. Suddenly, Miss Betsy could sense attention from others so she backed off. The basket came and mad Miss Betsy didn't even drop in a dime into the basket, as little Andre offered the whole fifty. A tear began to roll down Miss Betsy's cheek because she knew that the water would be cut off again tomorrow, for the third time this year.

"Your tail is mine when we get home." She whispered to Andre.

For some reason that meant nothing to Andre because for the first time in his life he made the half court shot that he had been attempting for years. It was a joyous occasion. He smiled as he heard the preacher say, "Believe God for the increase." What Miss Betsy didn't know is that little Andre had been listening every Sunday and he understood that giving was better than receiving and he was believing in God for a better place to live for his mother and him. They finished church and Andre was excited because he knew his seed had been planted, and they headed home, back to the number one crime location in the city. Miss Betsy saw life fading before her eyes but Andre saw the angels hovering over for a brighter day. Before they could stop the old brakeless car his mom told him to stay in the car. She went into the house and came out with a clothes hanger and beat poor little Andre like never before, in front of the house on the street. Andre slept in the car that night but the blood that poured down his arms and back became a sacrifice for his tithing that day.

The next day, Andre went to school with the blood on his clothes and no one seemed to notice or care. He had nothing to eat that morning and when lunch came there was nothing either. This wasn't that bad because there had been many days when Andre had given his lunch or even shared half his peanut butter and jelly sandwich. So that day lunch became an offering session for the little man of God. There were 34 kids in his class but at some point in time Andre had shared food with 28 of them. So the whole class pitched in that day to give Andre enough food to take home just in case his situation got worse. Andre went home that day not fearing, but praying that his mom would be ok. Andre was tough and knew he would be ok. He had become immune to pain because of his environment, so he sought joy through church. When he walked in the door, he sat down and read Philippians 4, "But my God shall supply all your need..." Tears began to roll down his face as he realized that no water was available once again. His mom came in at 5:00 p.m. to wash up and get ready for her second job at 7:00 pm. She called Andre's name,

"Yes ma'am," he replied.

"Come here, boy"

Andre came and sat down. "Andre I lost my full time job today, and I don't know if I can keep you anymore. I've done all I can to raise you, and I'm weak Andre." She wept as a baby as she reached out for her son." I'm so sorry for yesterday baby. Please forgive me?"

Andre nodded as if all was ok. "Mom, can I talk?"

"Go ahead baby."

"Mom what you are seeing is not what's going on. Mom the preacher said we are to walk by faith and not by sight. He said that God was our source and provision, not our job. I heard him, mommy. He said to be strong, always knowing that God is near. Mommy, I sowed yesterday for the first time, my very own first time. Mommy, do you tithe?" She wiped her tears and shook her head no. She had more pressing issues on her mind.

"Mom, listen just this once. I do know some things. The Bible says that if you tithe God will open up the windows of heaven and pour you out a blessing. Don't you want to be blessed?"

"Yes, baby."

"It's only ice cream money, Andre explained."

"What Dre?"

"Ten cents, that's what the cheap Popsicle sticks cost, ten cents. Anybody can do that mommy."

She started to lift her head as a sign of hope then fear set back in and she lowered it. "Anybody but me, Andre, anybody but me. Andre I told you I lost my job and I can't even keep the water on."

Andre jumped up and walked around the broken table. He took two steps to the window and looked out. He cracked a smile as if he knew that everything would be ok. Mommy don't give up; God is with us. You can't give me away."

She gave him a hug and said, "I have to go my other job now."

"Okay mommy, but remember, I gave yesterday and God doesn't forget mommy." Andre went into the one bedroom room and looked into the mirror. "God you will supply all my needs." That night Andre slept like a baby knowing that good was around the corner. He had a dream in his sleep that his mom was cleaning with gold slippers on. In the morning he took a bottle of his mom's special cleaning solution to school with him. He went into the principal's office but the receptionist told Andre he needed to go to class. As she grabbed his hand to escort him out, she felt the whelp on his arm. She raised his sleeve and saw the deep lashes.

"Poor boy, what has happened?" Wait here while I find Mr. Kelly." She escorted him into Mr. Kelly's office and showed him the wounds. Mr. Kelly whispered to the secretary to call the child abuse agency and she left the room as Mr. Kelly asked Andre what he needed.

"I need to talk to you, Mr. Kelly."

"I'm listening, Andre."

"I've got something that will change your life. Are you tired of this gum all over the school and these graffiti paintings?"

"Why sure I am."

"Well I can get it off for you. I have a special cleaner that my mom makes and it cleans everything. No stain can stay."

"That's good son, but what is going on with your arms. What happened to you?"

"Oh that's nothing Mr. Kelly, I ran through some briars."

"Andre are you sure?"

"Yes sir, I do it all the time."

"Briars, in the projects?"

"Oh no sir, got a cousin in the country. They have land and trees."

"Are you lying to me, Andre?"

"Maybe I am sir, maybe I'm not, but I'm here for the cleaner. If you want to help me Mr. Kelly, let my mom clean this school up."

"Andre, we already have a janitorial staff."

"Yeah, but the school is still not clean."

Mr. Kelly looked at his arms and said, "So this is how I can help you, huh? What is your Mom's phone number?"

"She doesn't have a phone but I can tell here to come see you tomorrow."

"Okay son, you do that." So Andre went home with eagerness. He missed the bus on purpose and dribbled his basketball all the way home. When he got home his mom was already there, which was unusual.

"Mom I've got you at job."

"Andre, what are you talking about?"

"Mom, I found you a place to work."

"Where Dre?"

"At the school. I talked to the principal and told him you could get the paint off the walls and the gum off the floor. He said for you to come tomorrow."

"Andre are you sure?"

"Yes mom, positive."

So the next morning Miss Betsy drove herself and Andre down to the school with the oil leaking and the muffler smoking. She went into the office to talk to Mr. Kelly.

"Miss, I want to talk to you about the bruises on Andre's arms first."

She bounced up as if Andre had lied to her. "What bruises?" she screamed.

"Ma'am have you not seen your son's arms? He said he got them from briars and I hope for everyone's sake that is true."

She calmed herself and agreed that Andre wouldn't lie. In all these years she thought within herself that her son had never lied once, but he did this one time to save her.

"So can you clean, ma'am?"

"Yes, sir, I can."

"Well, I will give you a small job to try as contract work and pay you on Friday, and we will go from there."

Friday rolled around and Miss Betsy got paid extra because of the amount of work she did. It was just enough to get her water turned back on and get her car fixed. Little did she know God had other plans. Sunday rolled around and tithe and offering time came. Andre looked at his mom and she looked at him. Mom you are going to give God back his popsicle right? She held her head in shame. She had figured the bills and the tithe was the exact amount it cost to repair the car. What do I do, she thought? No car, no job. Then a still voice said to her, "No tithe, no window." She immediately knew what had to be done. She broke into sobs as she wrote out her first tithe check. She knew that she couldn't withhold the Popsicle from God anymore. Just a dime per dollar she thought. Andre smiled as he saw her write the check out because he knew that God would provide. He leaned over to his mom and said, "okay mom." For the first time in her life she felt the same. All things will work for the good, she thought.

Miss Betsy went up to the school Monday to collect her cleaning supplies when Mr. Kelly stopped her. "Miss Betsy, that was one heck of a job you did getting rid of that graffiti. Do you know that the area superintendent saw what you did and he wants to give you a contract for all the schools in the county?" Betsy screamed "hallelujah" and fell to her knees. "All because I gave you the popsicle God. Thank you Jesus!!"

Mr. Kelly laughed and asked if she wanted the job?

"I'll start today."

No ma'am you can't. You have to meet with the state school board and work out a contract."

"Ok, she said. So Miss Betsy met with the board that Wednesday and sat down. They offered her the entire district with the possibility of the state. Miss Betsy's first contract was for $62,000, a big jump from the $14,000 she was making. Andre went on to get a scholarship to play Division One Basketball and he turned down the NBA to become a preacher. Miss Betsy got contracts for four states on the east coast making over a million dollars a year. She now travels to churches teaching and preaching the power of giving popsicles to God. She laughs every time she gives her tithe and offering and says, "God, you sure do like a lot of ice cream." She since has opened several facilities for those economically lacking and serves them ice cream all year round, proclaiming, "All God wants is a popsicle."

CONCLUSION

There is a spirit that attaches itself to money once in the hands of an individual. Either you're controlling money, or money is controlling you, no in betweens. Either you are chasing money or money is chasing you, no in betweens. Tithing is a continuous reminder that God is blessing you and a reminder of who your source is. Think about it. You tithe every time you get an increase. Increases come from God. So He gives you multiple chances to worship him, to thank him, to celebrate him and to have communion with him. This is giving you an opportunity to chase God's face instead of chasing Ben Franklin's face. <u>Every time I give it connects me to an unlimited source.</u> Deuteronomy 28 says obedience brings blessing, disobedience curses. God says He rewards obedience and Abraham knew this. So he tithed knowing his source. He spoke boldly in Genesis 14:22-23, "I will lift up my hands to the Most High God, possessor of heaven and earth."

Abraham had figured it out; he knew who his source was. He knew how to go before the Lord in thanksgiving.

He knew who gave him the strength to win in battle. Since he understood this he said, "I will not take anything that is-not mine. Anything that God didn't give me."

Abraham said that no man could ever say he made him rich. I love that because it's profound. How many people would turn down money just to do it God's way? Very few; actually most Christians go astray because of the pursuit of money. Not Abraham. He knew in his heart that God was his source and when God spoke a word he believed him. That's why the Bible said God counted it as righteousness unto him. The Bible says he was <u>fully persuaded.</u> If I could get twelve fully persuaded Christians we could change the world. I didn't say a million only twelve. That's all Jesus selected. Here's a secret to unlimited vision. Think on the promise day and night, the promise for vision. See in your spirit God downloading information that will allow you to change the world. God desires to fill us with His wisdom so that we can talk like Him, act like Him and give Him glory in the earth.

Tithing was never meant to be a legalistic act. It was always meant to be an act of obeying God. A spirit-led act. There is still a lot of work that needs to be done to advance His kingdom, and the time is now. I encourage you to tap into the power of a dime, the power that lies within the decision of your will. Search your heart. If you really love God, will giving him ten percent of what is already His hurt you? Will you decide to release your faith today for God's vision? Your future is bright and awaits you. I hope you make the decision to see it. I hope that you have an open heart and are receptive to what God has to say and wants to impart into your life through the principle of tithing.

If you are a male (reading this book) and consider yourself to be a man, it is imperative that you take heed to the principles discussed in this book. There is nothing worse than a woman who goes to church and the man stays at home and thinks he's a man because he works. A real man loves only are you robbing God but you are robbing your wife and children of the proper vision to lead. You are not in place to lead based upon God's insight for your life. Therefore you are taking your family through issues that could otherwise be avoided if you tapped into the principles given. I encourage you to find a deeper personal relationship with your creator so that He may give you the proper strength to guide your family in the direction that He desires for your life. A woman will never love a man to her full capabilities more than her ability to see him love God. The day that you begin to focus on him and his will for your life your family will truly be blessed.

Understanding the tithe is so important. It is critical that you understand it not only for the benefits it gives you but what it does for God. Tithing is God's way to advance his kingdom and get his work done in the earth. The church is becoming the world's last hope for the world as we know it. Our youth are going astray at a rapid pace. Grown men are chasing a dollar not knowing that the church has answers. It is up to the church (the people) to carry out God's assignment here on the earth. It won't get done if we don't start with the fundamental basic, which is tithing. Let's be realistic, without money the church cannot get things done, and it makes God look poor. How can a God who dwells in a place where the pavement is made of gold be made to look like a beggar? This only happens when his people fail to do their part in the earth's realm. God wants His house to be filled with gold. He doesn't have a problem with his children being rich but not at the expense of His house suffering or at the expense of you making money your master. When the people would make sacrifices in the Old Testament many times God would tell them to bring it in gold. God would dress the priests in the finest jewels. Why? He is an extravagant God. He desires the best of everything. If the church is supposed to be a representation of God here on the earth then why should it be any different? Yes, I understand that the brick and mortar building is not the actual church but it is still a symbolic representation of God. If we the people are the actual church then it is still a disgrace unto God that we allow his mission not to be done in excellence.

God is tired of leaking roofs, outdated seats, and baked goods sales to pay light bills. God is a God of excellence and expects his church, its leaders and the congregants to have the same spirit. The Bible says Daniel had an excellent spirit, and that is the spirit he expects of his children. If you are attending church and not giving your tithe then, yes, you are robbing God of what belongs to him. How am I robbing God if he owns it all? The Bible says God gave man dominion over the earth. So for God to get anything done here he has to do it through you. Dominion on earth has been given to man. You should pray and ask the Lord to lead you to a good church where there is a man (or woman) of God who feeds you the word, and is a visionary. Upon that place you should bring God His tithe so that His kingdom may go forth. There are people who will never hear the good news of the Gospel if you don't tithe. If it hurts you to tithe, then you really need to question your relationship with God. Do you really have a right relationship with God or money? I have never seen anyone become worse off from tithing. So don't get mad when the pastor asks you to give. He is doing his job as a high priest. If he is not a man of God then you have to make a spiritual judgment call as to why you are attending the church.

Don't stay at a church if the pastor is corrupt just so you can condemn him. You need to get into a church where the word of God is going forth and the pastor is an upright individual. You should never sow your tithe into dead ground. Understand that you are not giving your money to the pastor, but to the work of God. The pastor is just the vessel that the Lord uses to usher up the tithe unto him. However, the pastor should also be the visionary for God's people of that church, not the usher board or deacons. The congregation is there to help serve the man of God not pull him down. If the congregation focuses on uplifting the Man of God then he can focus on his appointed duty as pastor to serve the congregation. The devil has polluted the Gospel to the point where people would rather gamble away Gods money than release it to Him to advance his kingdom.

The word on the street asks, "Why you would take your money down to those money-hungry preachers?" Don't be stupid and miss your blessing over a lack of knowledge. Discover the truth for yourself. Once you release the tithe, it is God's obligation to open the window for your vision. When you think you are releasing the tithe to man you will begin to question what is being done with the money. Do your part, which is to give God the tenth and he will deal with the rest. If you are under good leadership the man of God should be a good steward over the things of God and do as God has instructed him. It is not your responsibility to stay up making phone calls to Sister Jane to gossip about how much money you gave. Have you called the president lately to ask what is being done with your tax money? You are giving unto God therefore you need to release man and hold God responsible. The gospel is free but the means in which to get it out are not. Television, radio, mortgage payment, light bill, water bill all cost money. Don't be so naive as to believe just because God is supposed to be at church that everything is free. The church has bills just like everyone else, if not more. So the next time you are questioning where the money is going be sure to thank God that the lights are on in the church. God desires that you be a blessing to others. That blessing begins with the dime. The simple ten cents of a dollar begins the process of vision so that you may see where to sow the offering for your harvest. Your time is now to go to the next level of living. Let God elevate your thinking and your bank account with supernatural insight into his world.

The tithe is Gods gateway to vision. Tithing has been one of the most rewarding experiences in my life. I encourage you to come into the land of endless possibilities.

My Prayer

This is my prayer for you. Father thank you for allowing revelation knowledge to flow through this individual. Thank you for allowing them to fully understand your desire for tithing. Thank you for purifying their heart so that they may hear your voice and obey your commands. Thank you for the insight, wisdom and witty ideas being poured into their spirit as they read. Move in their life mightily God for applying the principle of the tithe. You are the Most High God. Splendid and wonderful in all your glory. Show and guide them in the proper direction in every step of their life.

Let no confusion or destruction come about them, for you are rebuking all evil for their sake. I speak the abundant life of Christ into this individual now, that you may demonstrate your goodness, grace, and mercy through them. I pray that you're anointing rest upon them, so that harvests come plentiful. In Jesus name Amen.

TITHE CONFESSION

Lord I thank you for your word and your faithfulness. I thank you for life and life more abundantly. I thank you that you have my wellbeing in mind and that you are my creator. As my father I thank you for your obligation to provide for me. I thank you that I understand the tithe and I take great joy in releasing it unto you, Lord. I rejoice in bringing unto you your goods that in return, you may endow me with your vision. As I give my tithe I command the windows of heaven to open and pour me out a blessing as you promised in your word. I will not hold the accursed thing. The tithe is devoted. It belongs to you, God. I'm thankful that I do not have to try to make it on my own because you are there for me and provision belongs to me. Continue to provide for me Lord as I submit my will and my possessions unto you. Cleanse my heart to be more like you in every way. I will be obedient to what you have spoken unto me and I thank you. I thank you that you are rebuking the devourer for my sake. I thank you that you care enough about me to correct me. Move in a mighty way in my life to cause me to prosper today. I am walking in good success, divine health, and a sound mind. I prosper in all that I do because I serve the Most High God. Release an anointing for vision God, that I might have sweat-less victories in my life.

QUESTIONS ABOUT THE TITHE

I wanted to take questions about the tithe and answer them. Over the years I have heard every kind of question from A to Z. These questions were accumulated from non church members, church members, Bible scholars, and theologians.

1. Is it false doctrine to convince Christians that God wants them to pay tithes instead of teaching the importance of Giving?

I do not feel tithing should be a matter of coercing an individual rather that teaching them what God has to say about tithing. I agree that giving needs to be taught throughout the body of Christ as Paul preached it. However in teaching giving you must start with the basics and the basics of giving is teaching the tithe.

2. Why is it that preachers are the only ones to benefit from tithes and offerings and no one else from their church? Is this Biblical, if so, what chapter and verse?

Many have become frustrated with what they feel is the abuse of the tithe. The tithe should not be used as a blank check to furnish unlimited lifestyles. However, I find it hard to believe that preachers are the only ones to benefit from the tithe. First and foremost, you must remember that the preacher is the vessel who ushers up the tithe, but you should not see your tithe as going to him, but going to the work of the Lord. If you are giving and looking at what the preacher is wearing, wondering if your $100 a month paid for it, you are in error. It is not free for the church lights, water, and phone to stay on. The churches bills have to be paid. In addition, everything in the house of God should be done in excellence. The tithe allows this to be possible. Also the Bible says is it wrong for a man who has sown spiritual things unto us to reap carnal things. One should be allowed to earn an income for a suitable living if he has dedicated his life to God for the serving of his people.

See scriptures: 1st Corinthians 9:11-14, Numbers 18

3. Abraham paid tithes once, there are three different tithes taught under the law, and what we do today does not resemble any of the Biblical teaching, why?

The fact that the Bible gives only one instance of Abraham tithing does not mean he tithed only once. That's like saying Daniel probably fasted only once. That is an assumption we cannot make and you must look at the entire walk of Abraham. The bible clearly tells us his grandson Jacob even tithed. That was not an accident which tells me Abraham fulfilled his part of the covenant in passing it on to his children and more than likely that was not his only tithe. You are correct that there were three tithes practiced under the law. The tithe has always been a tenth of your gross. That was established by God. The use of the tithe was also established. If the way that the tithe is used today are within the guidelines of this then I think God is ok with   it.

Remember the tithe is for the Church, church clergy, poor, widow, foreigners, strangers, and orphans.

4. Why should Christians pay tithes since it is Old Testament and under the law?

Tithing is not just Old Testament; it is also New Testament. Not only is it New Testament but it is also a Biblical principle that God put in the earth for those who believe on him to be blessed. Tithing is a command by God and the only principle in the Bible, God said to test me on the issue. Also note in the book tithing was passed on from Melchizedek to Jesus. Also noted in this book Abraham tithed 430 years before the law. Tithing is a principle that continued beyond the cross. See: Genesis 14:18, Deuteronomy 12:11, Leviticus 27:31, Malachi 3:10, Hebrews 7.

5. In the book of Malachi 3, who is God talking to? Is this a valid scripture to use in the church today?

Good question, but just because something is in the Old Testament does not mean you throw it out of the Bible. God was talking to the Levite priests and the Israelites. However, this scripture is still very valid because it allows you to see God's thoughts on tithing, the causes and effects of tithing which still hold true today.

6. Are Christians cursed if they don't pay tithes and will they go to hell?

This is a two part question. First, Malachi 3 tells us that we are cursed with a curse. Those are the words of God. There are many things that died at the cross with Jesus, which removed us from the curse of the law. However the scriptures tell us that tithing went beyond the cross, which means this, would still apply today. Also in Joshua chapter seven, Achan had stolen from God the accursed thing. Accursed meaning dedicated or devoted thing. The whole camp was cursed because of this theft. I see the tithe as also a devoted thing. This is why I personally wouldn't want to be equal partners in a business with a non tither. Nor would I want someone in leadership at my church that wasn't tithing. As far as going to hell, I don't see any Biblical context directly related to the tithe and hell, nevertheless Matthew 25 lets us know that the poor steward did go to hell for poor management of God's money. This is something you as an individual would have to answer for on your judgment day. Why you did or did not tithe God will judge your heart and actions.

7. If I am struggling financially with my bills should I tithe or should I pay my bills?

This is a question that many wonder about. The Bible tells us in Matthew 6 that God knows our needs before we even ask. In saying this, it is God's responsibility to take care of you as a born again believer (which makes you a citizen in the kingdom of God). If you believe that God will provide, then you need to bring to him the tithe and do what you can on your end. The tithe releases vision so that you can see where you have been going wrong. Every step toward self-sufficiency is a step away from God. I would much rather bring the tithe and rely on God rebuking the devourer than on my own knowledge and works. Relying on God doesn't mean I set back and do nothing. I still need to do all I can in the natural to go forward while believing that God will bring the increase.

8. Why do churches say pay tithes off your gross?

The Bible says that you give the tithe of all thine increase, not part. God owns it all, so when he asks you to bring him something he wants what he asked for as if he owns it all, because he does. When they asked Jesus if he paid taxes, Jesus said to obey the law and give unto Cesar what belongs to him. God has nothing to do with the government taxes. He is not concerned about that. He wants ten percent of everything he gave you the strength to produce. Not ten percent of what's left after you've acknowledged everyone else.

See: Genesis 14:20, Deuteronomy 14:22

9. Why is there a difference in how Mosaic Law taught tithes and how it is practiced in churches today?

I personally think that part of your answer lies within your question. The way that tithing is taught is a customary or cultural thing regarding the Jewish customs of that time. What God has told us is how much the tithe is, who to give it to, what it is for, where to bring it and why. This is the information that we need to apply today and I think this is being done in the proper fashion by most churches that believe in tithing.

10. "Tithes, tithing, tithe" appears in the Bible 40 times depending upon your translation, yet "give, gives, giving, gave" appears over 800 times; why is there so much emphasis placed on the lesser part than the one that is mentioned the most? Tithing is the first principle in understanding giving. If you can not obey God with the ten percent surely you wont obey him with the hundred percent. If God cannot trust you to give the tithe how can he trust you to give at all? For those who give freely, that is good but always remember that obedience is better than sacrifice. Are you giving to   try to

make yourself feel better or are you giving because the spirit of God asked you to and your heart is right?

FRED WYATT MINISTRIES

This book this is one of over 20 Biblical prosperity books the Lord has placed in my spirit for the Body of Christ. I ask that you stay plugged into this ministry that it may help guide you in the area Satan pulls most, finances. If this book has blessed you I ask that you pray about sowing into this ministry. The ground is fertile and the funds will be used for Godly exploits. I believe God will do great things in your life. I also believe God will make a covenant of increase with those who bless and link up with this ministry. I am excited that you have now embarked into a new arena with God. God will do his part if you do your part. Please do not let money run you. Don't make the mistake of letting him bless you and the blessing overwhelms you and you forget who gave the blessing. That is imperative. Stay strong and tune in for the next wave of revelation. God Bless. Love your brother in Christ-Fred Wyatt.

CONTACT US

For more information about Fred Wyatt Ministries please write to us or visit us on the worldwide web at:

Web: www.fredwyatt.com
Email: *Coming Soon*

All donations can be made online or mailed to the following address: P.O. Box 750 Mechanicsville, Virginia 23111